This England

THIS ENGLAND

By

MARY ELLEN CHASE

NEW YORK

THE MACMILLAN COMPANY

1936

PRINTED IN THE UNITED STATES OF AMERICA
BY THE STRATFORD PRESS, INC., NEW YORK

To

COLLEGE HOLT

AND THOSE WITHIN ITS HOSPITABLE GATES,

IN APPRECIATION OF MANY HOURS

AROUND AN ENGLISH FIRE

This royal throne of kings, this scepter'd isle,
This earth of majesty, this seat of Mars,
This other Eden, demi-paradise,
This fortress built by Nature for herself
Against infection and the hand of war,
This happy breed of men, this little world,
This precious stone set in the silver sea,
Which serves it in the office of a wall
Or as a moat defensive to a house,
Against the envy of less happier lands,
This blessed plot, this earth, this realm, this England.

SHAKESPEARE, *Richard II.*

Foreword

The thirteen sketches which comprise this book have been written during the last months of a two years' residence in England. They are now offered to whoever may be interested as a proof of gratitude for the innumerable blessings of such a sojourn. They are meant to chronicle various impressions of the English as a people,—of their traditions, their habits and manners, their predilections and aversions—and to present a picture, necessarily inadequate, of their unparalleled countryside. Like all impressions they are personal and individual, dictated, as is always the case, by the person who receives them as well as by those who unconsciously give. They are meant to be desultory rather than summary or conclusive, to suggest, perhaps to recall, rather than to inform. And they have been written in deepest thanks for English friendliness and courtesy, particularly for that accorded me in the village of Grantchester, and in appreciation of an incomparably beautiful country,—yes, even of English weather!

MARY ELLEN CHASE.

Burnt Close
Grantchester, Cambridge, England.

July, 1936.

Contents

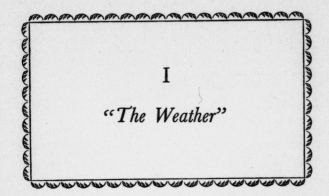

I

"The Weather"

I

As ALL know who read that estimable, matchless, and somewhat dull daily, the London *Times*, the weather of the British Isles is always accorded a position of respect, deference, and honour. It is invariably placed near the middle of the paper on the left-hand sheet immediately opposite the Court Circular which invariably occupies the right. During a two years' sojourn in England and a regular if not daily perusal of the *Times* I have known it to be moved from its place but once. That was upon the occasion of the death of King George V, when even it gave way to matters, for the time being, of more serious importance.

No one who has lived for two years under its omnipotent sway would wish it moved from its high station or question its inalienable right to its position. For, one gradually comes to understand, it has played a far greater part in the upbringing of the

3

nation than have the Norman Conquest, Magna Charta, the Puritan Rebellion, or the Great Reform Bill. Through its countless combinations and permutations, through its manifold ramifications, it has moulded English character and shaped British destiny. Nor could one wish any alteration, any intrusion of the familiar, in the deliberate, dignified, and wholly literary style in which observations upon it are couched. Even the movements of the King himself from Buckingham to Windsor, from Sandringham to Balmoral, the audiences which His Majesty has been graciously pleased to grant this dignitary and that, are not more elegantly described:

A deep depression off the Hebrides is slowly moving south-eastward while a secondary disturbance is steadily advancing from the direction of the Azores. Weather will be dull and rather cold in most districts with cold showers of rain or sleet. Snow is likely to fall in Scotland and the north of England. Bright intervals are possible though not probable on the south coast. Further outlook: Unsettled.

The wireless announcer, who at six o'clock halts all late teas with his decorous recital and at nine-thirty depresses or merely confirms the minds of thousands of his listeners from Hastings to John O'Groats, only complements the dignity of the press in the finality of his measured tones:

Further outlook: Unsettled in most districts.

It is this further outlook which, with its sickening pang of hope deferred, is so dampening to the spirits of the foreigner, especially of the American who has been stupid (or wise) enough to spend some time in England. His weather, whatever it may be, is *not* a national phenomenon. He knows that after a brief period of honest, downright rain, he can usually rely upon a long succession of bright days. He does not need to approach picnics or long drives in the country with suspicion or qualms or simply with resignation and a raincoat. Through long and, for the most part, reassuring experience with the meteorology governing *his* weather, he is accustomed to depend upon decent treatment; in other words, he is used to it, much as he is used to ice in his drinking-water at table and to heat in his living-room. If he contemplates a stay of any length on an island, which, just as it affords him little ice and less heat, can guarantee him nothing as to the weather he must tolerate (except that most of it will be intolerable), he would best stock well up in advance on composure, fortitude, and good humour.

II

After a winter in any part of the British Isles the American is no longer moved to pity of the Pilgrim Fathers through Mrs. Felicia Hemans's once moving description of Cape Cod in December. The breaking waves, the stormy sky, the darkness of the heavy night fade into nothingness after one has battled along the Cornish cliffs enveloped in a dense fog and literally pierced by the sharpest and wettest rain in the world; or crossed the high, bare Wiltshire downs in a wind that finds nothing to break its speed or alleviate its temperature; or listened in the dead of night to the shrieking gusts which tear across the Cambridgeshire fens, straight from Siberia, it seems, since there is not a hill to stay their way from Kamchatka to Norwich! On bitter January evenings this past winter, one of the worst England has known for years, after trying in vain by all the inadequate methods at the nation's disposal to raise the thermometer in a cellarless living-room to sixty degrees, I have many times exclaimed with all the irritation which only a pampered American can feel

6

that Cape Cod at its worst might well have looked
and felt like the Riviera to the Pilgrim Fathers!

An English winter like the one just past, when
January could boast of only thirty hours of sunshine
and when out of a succession of ninety days seventy
were rainy, has its confederates and accomplices.
There are, first of all, chilblains. These inflamma-
tions of toes, elbows, and fingers, amusing as they
may be to English doctors bent on higher matters,
are exasperating beyond words to the afflicted foreigner. To sit for hours in the University Library
at Cambridge, where your British neighbour throws
open two windows after you have surreptitiously
and desperately closed one; to remain, while you
are struggling to concentrate on your reading, in a
perpetual state of subconscious indecision as to
whether or not to scratch your offending members;
to shiver *in toto* while you burn and itch *in partibus
tribus*—this daily occupation demands more resignation and humour than is the capital of most steam-
heated Americans. The woollen underwear which
one must wear or perish harbours and transmits its
manifold vexations; two steaming cups of tea at
four o'clock afford but incomplete and temporary
solace; by four-thirty the darkness has fallen, and
English lighting everywhere is woefully inadequate.

By the time you have trudged homeward in wet boots to a dinner of boiled potatoes, brussels sprouts, and the good, solid, virtuous roast beef of old England, eaten in a dining-room at 54° Fahrenheit, your stock is several degrees below par. It drops still lower as you face the inevitable prospect of crawling into bed between icy linen sheets in a fireless room!

Nor does this weeping endure but for a night with the Psalmist's surety of joy on the morrow. In spite of the fact that the evenings are often deceptive, there is no assurance whatsoever that the following day will alter or improve the situation. English moonlight in winter is untrustworthy to precisely the same degree that it is beautiful. It suffuses the wet, mist-hung fields, brings the hayricks into sharp relief, dims the stars with its radiance. I have seen numberless miserable days transformed at early evening into nights that Italy might envy, only at some undiscovered hour before dawn to reassert themselves and resume their former cheerlessness. Indeed, there are a good nine chances out of ten that the following day will be only a slightly dissimilar copy of the one preceding—the same lowering skies, the same driving slants of rain with possible interludes of capricious and languid sunshine, the same cold winds from any one of four directions, perhaps some morning and evening fog to add perilous variety to the incessant program of at least three months of the year. Queen Elizabeth's motto, *Semper eadem,* although it is commonly granted a loftier connotation, might well have been applied to the weather under which she reigned for forty-five years!

It is this dismal monotony of discomfort which seems at times so unbearable, these sudden changes from rain to weak sunlight, from mist to cloud, set about and enclosed, however, by a stout wall of comparative certainty. The mood of the day may have its tricks, but its outstanding temper will vary little. One longs for something immoderate, extreme, even violent—a hurricane, a blizzard, a tornado—to rouse into sharp activity this all-pervading chill and dullness. But English weather, like the people it has made, cherishes an aversion to anything cataclysmic or extreme. Both are classic in their strict adherence to the tenet of *Nothing in excess*. It pursues its solitary way, even in its very unevenness. Its rare and beautiful frosts, which throughout most of the country take the place of snow, give way to mud, the most adhesive in the western world; its rains, seldom torrential, alternate with brief periods of wan sunlight; its winds shriek but rarely demolish;

its damp cold penetrates to the very marrow, but with complete decorum usually stops just short of freezing.

If perchance a few sharp days of unwonted temperature spread a thin layer of uncertain ice over the submerged fens and the shallowest of streams and lakes, the population at large turns out to view the skating. If a rare snowfall comes, village children beg politely at one's back door for some extra shovels-full from one's garden to swell their small supply for snow-men and snow-balls. These are stupendous events, chronicled by press and wireless throughout the nation. No one thinks of chronicling the dogged human endurance which persists from Westmoreland to Sussex from late November to late February. Perhaps at that it is not endurance. It may be instead that old Dr. Johnson was but characterizing the nature of his own countrymen when he declared in *Rasselas* that that which cannot be repaired is not to be regretted.

III

Small wonder that the English are not a prophetic people, since from birth to death they are daily inured to taking their weather as they find it. The most glorious of spring and summer mornings, the sun rising in a cloudless sky, give no proof or even sign that the afternoon will be fine. Meredith did well to have Richard and Lucy meet in the early morning by the river! One soon learns, indeed, to grasp the truth that the brighter and clearer the morning, the more portentous for the afternoon. There is a saying on the North Devonshire coast which I have proved too many times not to recognize its validity: "If you can see the sun on the Welsh shores in the morning, look out for rain by noon." Understanding of this fact has surely given rise to the current salutations concerning the weather. One seldom, if ever, hears, "It's a nice day" from the lips of the English. Instead they wisely comment solely on the brief hours at hand: "It's a bright morning." "A fine afternoon." "A pleasant evening."

The most auspicious token of a fine day and evening lies in a dark, sulky dawn, the clouds low over the chimney-pots of one's neighbours, the fields drenched in mist and rain. The world looks dull enough in all conscience. Notwithstanding these symptoms, however, unless one of those durable depressions off the Hebrides or Scandinavia is moving forward or a secondary disturbance from Ireland or the Azores is claiming prolonged attention, there is a fair chance that by ten o'clock the mists will disappear before the sun and the pale blue English sky become at last visible. The English sunshine is close, benign, friendly, lying in warm, soft light over the greenest land in the world, in winter as well as in summer. Like the people it shines upon it is never lavish, always holding in abeyance its richest fruits. But nowhere is it more appreciated, because of its very reserve.

It is easy to become convinced, however, that England actually tires of too much sun. When a rare and strong "anti-cyclone belt" (the most welcome phrase in the language to one sojourning here!) remains for days on end over this island, as it has for some summers past, bringing days of real warmth ripening into heat, the native Britisher does not seem really at home. He has certain well-worn adjectives descriptive of his discomfort. The air, he says at breakfast over his *Times,* is "thundery" (though thunder seldom comes) "most oppressive"; the weather is "tiresome", "most relaxing". One surmises he would welcome those occasional spurts of rain which mark most of his days, even the fairest. He is more at ease under his familiar, moody skies than under those that suggest other lands with which he is voluntarily unfamiliar. For your average or typical Englishman, in spite of English adventuring and colonization, is at heart no ardent traveller. The stakes must be large or the situation extreme which will set him often a-journeying to far places. He does travel, it is true, but one suspects that he does it largely to be confirmed, like Wordsworth, in a new sense of the glory and superiority of home. He likes best the things to which he has been long used—his compact trees, his own fireside, his walks over English stiles through English fields under his own low-hung clouds.

The English do not wait on their weather. If they did, they would do little else. Nor do they disregard it, it being too much a part of them for such neglect. They forbear it when it demands forbearance and enjoy it whenever they are allowed to do so. An English holiday crowd is the best-natured in the world; Merrie England nowhere displays itself to such good advantage as in a summer rain. I have seen swarms of school children in the New Forest happily standing under convenient trees or batting cricket-balls about in the mud. On the sands at Brighton or Weymouth, Blackpool or Weston-super-Mare good-humoured women eat sprats and Bath buns under affluent umbrellas, while their offspring in bathing-suits ladle wet sand into buckets, glad of the sun when it comes out, patient in the rain when it stays hidden. And when at twilight the skies clear as they often do, the green fields and lanes are traversed by both town and country—old men out to take the freshly washed air, women glad of a stroll before bed-time, small boys at their eternal cricket, young folks in love walking naïvely with interlocked fingers. Their placid faces show no inroads from the day's showers or downpour as the case may be. They may call their weather beastly or wretched, depressing or tiresome, but they like it. They wear their mackintoshes gallantly and feel more at home in wet boots than in dry.

It is, in fact, this great good humour in the face of what would be unspeakable irritation to any other people, this imperturbation in the face of what is and must be, this taking matters as they find them with just enough good-tempered grousing to assert their rights as individuals, this inbred faith in things working out well enough in the long run—a careless, practical, quite unmystical faith—which mark the English as unique. They are as illogical as their weather and perhaps as incomprehensible. Surely it has played no small part in making them what they are; and just as surely it is meet and right that they should accord it the same friendly

14

respect which they accord the Court Circular in direct juxtaposition to it in the *Times:*

His Majesty the King was graciously pleased to grant this morning an audience to His Excellency, the Maharajah of Nagalaboo.

A deep depression from the North Atlantic is centred off the Hebrides and moving slowly southward.

IV

Once in Somerset at the close of a long, churlish day spent in walking in the vicinity of Wells and Glastonbury, I came upon a farm labourer resting beneath a hedge. He had thrown over his shoulders one of the coarse, brown grain-sacks which English labourers often carry to protect them against the exigencies of the weather, and was smoking his pipe in great content. The rain had well-nigh ceased; only the gentlest of showers was falling. The August cuckoo-pints were glowing red in the intricacies of the hawthorn, and a thrush was singing. In the west the clouds had broken to reveal a clear sky and foretell a fine evening.

"Good-night," he called to me in the common

salutation of the country. "The rain's over, I'm thinking, and a fair night be upon us."

"Not too good a day," I said, with disappointment still within me.

"That's a fact," he said. "It takes all kinds to make a summer, that it do."

II

English Sources of American
Irritation

I

To THE American who dwells for a season within these stout and well-fortified coasts there are probably no such irritating people under the sun as are the English. Perhaps this fact lies in another, namely that because many of us are sprung from them, we expect them to be more like us than they are. The initial exasperation comes when we discover immediately that this is at once a complete and baffling misconception. Our common language, the physical characteristics common to us both, many other elements of our common inheritance—all would seem to afford points of similarity between us. But these things have not resulted in resemblance or even in affinity. Three hundred years of a totally different environment and development have set us apart from them; and this must be coupled by the knowledge that each decade in their tight little island only serves to make them more uncompromisingly what they are.

In England all who are not English are foreigners. The term is not given in opprobrium; it is merely a fact, downright and inescapable. In England the American is a foreigner precisely as is the Jew, the Frenchman, and the Spaniard. The Englishman has no objection to foreigners, providing they remain what they are and do not attempt any approximation to him; in fact, the more they exhibit the most strongly marked peculiarities of their own countries, the more he respects and likes them. To the English any attempt to appear or any wish to become something other than what is prescribed by one's original nature is despicable, even dishonourable, simply because it is unnatural; and the wish or attempt to do violence to nature is diametrically opposed to the whole English character. The American may be laughable, extraordinary, incomprehensible, even ridiculous and absurd to the Englishman; nevertheless, he wants him solidly and substantially as he *is*, much as he wants his meat to taste of itself, his clothes to be made of good English stuff, and his house to be constructed without a lot of decoration to cover up its original English stability.

Once this basic, honest attitude is accepted by the American for precisely what it is, he should have no quarrel with it, exasperating as it may seem to him in the first vexatious weeks of its inception. There are, however, arising from it countless minor irritations which do not subside either into forbearance or amusement until some months or years of living among the English have done their work.

It is but fair to say at the outset that as a people Americans are prone to irritation, and never so much so as when away from home. This does not arise from innate temperament so much as from the habits and customs to which we have long been used. A high standard of efficiency and comfort in our daily living results naturally enough in an equally high standard of expectation and demand. When we find ourselves in a country in which too much efficiency is suspected and too much comfort scorned, in which no one has hurried for centuries or has the slightest notion of hurrying now, we are faced with the necessity of adapting ourselves to a point of view vastly irritating in itself. We may stay and suffer through the process of adaptation, or we may leave. It matters not a whit to the English.

II

First among the minor irritations of life in England are those which arise from domestic arrange-

ments. And in these I must say at once that I have
been most fortunate. The cottage in Cambridgeshire
which has been my home for two years is well built,
attractive, and artistically furnished. The variegated
old tiles which form its well-placed roof are fully as
picturesque as and far more cleanly than the thatch,
which delights the foreigner with its quaintness but
which, alas! often harbours other inmates than
those who dwell beneath it. Its rooms are well-
floored and easy to keep clean; its fireplace draws to
perfection; it is supplied with electric lights which
suffuse a fairly adequate if not radiant glow; its
bath-room has an ample window and a tub of white
enamel in pleasing contrast to the tin ones which are
still prevalent in both town and country; and it
boasts five radiators, which, although they do not
heat it according to American standards, help in
some slight degree to alleviate the all-pervading
chill. My housekeeper—for whom I praise heaven
hourly!—besides being intelligent and companion-
able, is an excellent cook and shares my own desire
for orderliness. Truly English lines have fallen unto
me in pleasant places!

And above all else, as a cause for gratitude, in my
bed-rooms the bureaus (or as they say in England the
chests or the *dressing-tables*) do not stand as they do

in nine out of ten English houses directly in front of the windows. This ugly phenomenon is one of the first things to strike the eye and annoy the imagination of the American traveller or sojourner. There they are, in themselves usually far from beautiful, with the backs of their ungainly mirrors directly visible to all who pass. In a drive from Liverpool to Cambridge a year ago my companion and I amused ourselves by counting bureaus thus placed. Before we had left the confines of Cheshire, we had reached the seven hundredth mark and thereupon gave ourselves up to the far more delightful scrutiny of the English countryside than which nothing on earth can be more lovely. The dwellings of high and low alike share in this peculiar taste. To those who wait outside the high gates of Buckingham Palace to see the Guards changed or to catch a chance glimpse of royalty, the royal bureaus are clearly in evidence smack against the royal windows!

To the foreigner at least there seems no adequate reason for this custom. Assuredly it brings acutely home to those dressing before the bureaus the most glaring of their facial defects; it quite summarily darkens the bed-rooms; it precludes the view of garden, of country, or of street; and it necessitates a nightly struggle with the bureau if one wishes a good supply of fresh air. One of the best of modern English architects has stated in a recent book the simplest explanation: "A bedroom has a bed, a night-table, a dressing-table in front of the window, and so on. Why? Merely because a bedroom has always been furnished in this way."

Nevertheless, grateful as I am for this and manifold other blessings, there *are* irritations even in a comparative Elysium. English kitchen sinks, even in fairly modern houses, are seldom constructed with forethought as to the backs and legs of those who bend over them. My English stove, which supposedly heats the house and the water and in reality does neither, is small, squat, and stubborn both in appearance and in personality. Two weeks of fast-diminishing patience were required at the beginning of our acquaintance before I at last learned to master its moods against early mornings and Sundays when my housekeeper is not with me. This stove has nothing to do with the cooking. In contrast to most English kitchens, which possess coal ranges, the cooking in my house is accomplished with apparent ease on an ancient oil-burner in a tiny adjoining cook-room. My housekeeper at first declined my offer of an electric stove. She had never used one; she was not inclined to begin to use one; she had small patience with new gadgets; she had always used an oil-stove, and she felt more at home doing as she had always done. That, as the English say, was plainly that!

The drainage system of my cottage is for the most part above ground—that is, the pipes are open pipes through which the water from bath and kitchen sink alike runs into a small underground cess-pool placed too near the house for pleasant contemplation. My bread is delivered at my back door by the baker's boy, who holds it quite unwrapped against his somewhat unwashed shirt. Just as the water running through my uncovered drains sounds a merry, musical, reassuring sound, so does the bread-laden baker's boy look jaunty and picturesque as he hands me his very good bread. It is well, one learns, to dwell on this feature of unchangeable situations.

The almost complete absence of ice in England for any of the convenient purposes common in America is yet another source of domestic irritation. Ice simply is NOT, at least outside of the large and expensive London hotels and restaurants which make it their business to cater for foreigners. In a two years' sojourn here, during which I have driven for thousands of miles through town and country in every possible direction, I have never seen a load of ice; and it is quite safe to say that out of every ten thousand average homes not one possesses any sort of refrigeration. There is reason for this, of course, in that, except for two months in the summer and then not always, the climate is not warm. Moreover, town houses often have their kitchens and other "offices" under the level of the ground where milk, cream, and butter can be kept in decent condition. The chief reasons (perfectly sound from the English point of view) lie, however, in that, first, the English consider ice an extravagant and unnecessary commodity, and, second, that as a people they do not like cold foods or drinks.

When we decide that we can no longer survive in our cottage without ice, we betake ourselves in the car to the fishmonger in the nearest sizable town. This puzzled but always good-humoured man sells us a piece twelve cubic inches in size at the price of a shilling, wraps a sheet of brown paper around it, and watches us start homeward with the ice at our feet. When we reach home, we usually give ourselves up immediately to an orgy of lemonade since the life of ice on a warm English day is fleeting. Sometimes we have the foresight to place our languid lettuce on what remains so that the salad at dinner may remind us for a brief season of the conveniences of home.

Flies in England are tenacious insects largely because there is small discouragement of their activities. The temperature of the larder during the late spring and summer months is as congenial to them as elsewhere in an English home. The most common English fly, I was told by an inconsiderate entomologist at an inopportune moment, is the fruit fly, commonly employed in experiments in genetics because he breeds so rapidly. There may be windowscreens somewhere in England, but I have never seen one; and English windows are forever open, at least during the day, in all weathers and at all seasons. (The fresh air which Americans hold to be a sign of respectability during the hours of darkness is in England largely reserved for the hours of light.)

English wasps, however, encircle all the flies from the Isle of Wight to the Tweed with a sentimentalism akin to that of Uncle Toby in *Tristram Shandy!* For the wasp is the most completely domesticated creature of all English animal life. There is hardly a breakfast or lunch, surely never a tea, from May until October which is not copiously attended by wasps. They have a passion for marmalade, porridge, fruits and berries of all kinds, plum cake and cus-

tards. And as though bowls and plates of these com-
modities were lacking to them in the human touch,
they adore to explore one's fingers during the somewhat sticky process of spreading one's toast with
black currant jam. A nervous American woman with
an English wasp on her finger presents a problem-
atical as well as a humourous situation. Usually, to
the woman at least, the problem outweighs the
humour!

III

I have pondered for some minutes, pen in hand,
over whether or not the telephone service in England affords a domestic irritation; but I decide here
and now that, domestic or not, it deserves an inviolable space by itself. Recently I have determined
that, once I reach New York, I shall hasten to the
nearest telephone booth with numberless nickels
and spend them all in calling up every person I
know in that city merely for the satisfaction of a
good and immediate connection. The connection on
local calls, if made on one's own telephone, is toler-
able in England. But a nerve-racking situation presents itself, especially to the newcomer, if, having no
telephone of his own, he must procure his number

in a wayside telephone stand. He enters one of these boxes, which in the neighbourhood of towns are placed at about a mile, or in thickly settled communities, half a mile apart. With his two coppers (if he is wise, he will carry four or six) clenched tightly in his perspiring hand, he begins nervously to study both the odd mechanism before him and the directions governing its successful use. He discovers a slot for his coppers and two projecting buttons marked A and B. From the directions, which he reads carefully several times with increasing bewilderment, he ascertains that once he has lifted the receiver and heard one of two kinds of *BURR,* he is to drop his coppers and give his number. This is relatively easy. It is A and B who afford the difficulty. B, he reads, is not to be touched unless his call has failed to reach its destination, in the event of which a savage punch on B will, presumably, restore his coppers to him. The working of A is more erudite. He reads, "When you hear the voice of your correspondent, and NOT BEFORE, press button A and speak. Unless button A is pressed, you cannot be heard." The palpitating moments of standing in the stuffy box, ear to the receiver, fingers on A; the fear of not being able to recognize the voice of one's correspondent if, and when, it comes; the agony of misgiving as to whether your correspondent will wait for A to be punched (for curiously enough this pressing of button A is seemingly the one act in England which requires both haste and efficiency)—these are emotions calculated to make inroads even on the stoutest foreign nervous system.

But the heavy toll demanded by this process is as nothing compared to that involved in the completion of a trunk, or long distance, call. In the first place, in addition to the length of time always involved, one can never be certain that, if a call is put through to a London hairdresser on Bond Street, a dentist in Cavendish Square may not courteously answer. And yet the irritation subsequent upon this inaccuracy is a trifle in comparison to that engendered by the extreme politeness of the trunk operator. For, in addition to the first irritation, another crowds mercilessly upon the one who waits with the receiver at his ear—this other born of the recognition that one should be assuaged, not exasperated by politeness. The volatile, superabundant politeness of the Frenchman and the Spaniard may quite decently provoke irritation since it seems in itself a rôle easily assumed for the occasion and quite as easily shed. But this deliberate, sincere, deep-rooted, never shaken, stubborn courtesy of the English, in no one more apparent than in the trunk operator, surely should not merit exasperation. And yet, unfairly enough, it does that very thing.

"I am extremely sorry, madam," says the trunk operator, "to keep you waiting in this way. The line seems difficult to obtain this morning."

Another five minutes pass. You are perfectly aware that the rice pudding for lunch is burning in the oil-stove; but you are tied to the receiver. Again the trunk operator's quiet, unperturbed voice.

"I trust you will excuse this tiresome delay, madam. I assure you I am doing my utmost to put you through."

In addition to his virtue of politeness the trunk operator is possessed of yet another. He does not want you to spend your money recklessly. Unless you carefully tell him that you are ready, financially able, and eager to pay for a six-minute conversation, he will ruthlessly cut you off at the expiration of three minutes. You may be outlining a train schedule, ascertaining the time of a funeral, concluding the hour for a doctor's appointment—it makes no difference *what* you are talking about. The trunk operator's voice says, "Three minutes, please," and a desolation of silence ensues. Unless philosophy comes to your aid, other conversation is likely to follow, angry on your part, tranquil on his, once you have again secured him.

"You cut me off!"

"I'm sorry, madam, but your three minutes had elapsed."

"I wanted six minutes."

"I beg your pardon, madam, but unless you ask in advance for unlimited service, three minutes is the time allotted."

The conclusion to the whole weary matter is more unbearable than the matter itself. For as you draw the dry and overbrowned rice pudding from the oven, you are besieged by the uneasy consciousness that somehow you yourself have shown up to far worse advantage than the trunk operator or than the entire telephonic system of the British Isles!

IV

No one hurries as a practice in England. This meaningless, or even meaningful, activity is directly opposed to all that is most deeply rooted in the English character. A small, old compact country, the most inland of whose towns is within a half day's journey of the sea, whose roads, especially in the south, winding in and out between the hedgerows, make speed impossible to the motorist, whose villages have been half asleep for centuries, does not, cannot, indeed *will* not nurture undue haste of any sort. A composed past, a tranquil present, and an unperturbed faith in a steady, self-sufficient future —none of these breeds the desire for dispatch or urgency.

Moderation in all movements is the watchword of English life; and a climate which knows few extremes, no real heat in summer to encourage lassitude, no real cold in winter to instil energy, has admirably contrived to keep this golden mean. The Oxford and Cambridge undergraduates in training, who trot along the meadows by their respective rivers, give the impression rather of relaxation and pleasure than of any preparation for winning a race. Usually in pairs, they chat with each other, look about them, and in general suggest that wholesome enjoyment of sport for its own sake which is a national idea and ideal. Not for them the nervous intensity of the American youth bent on distinguishing his college and himself!

No one hurries in England. The farmer plods behind his blue cart and his slow horses, smoking his pipe; the grocer takes ample time and more to do up his parcels; Houses of Parliament suspend their activities to drink afternoon tea; and the guards who wave the last flags at Paddington or Waterloo as a signal for the trains to start do it slowly and deliberately as though a schedule had no relation whatsoever to a train.

These manners are innate, irrevocable, unalterable as is the weather and not infrequently, at least to the American, as irritating. His almost limitless country is not yet old; within his memory it was possessed of a frontier toward which the most adventurous of his countrymen were pressing. Its methods of life have been cleverly devised to suit its needs, not inherited and revered as tradition. Its broad, straight highways stretch from ocean to ocean, luring the eye for miles upon miles and offering the exhilaration of speed at the maximum safety. Its climate for at least nine months of the year, except in its southern States, is invigorating. Its idea of life is to be up and doing lest a better man overtake the idler; its schools overteach the doctrines of ambition and success; and its churches number among their favourite hymns, "Work for the Night Is Coming".

It makes little difference whether or not the American personally subscribes to these methods and tenets. He has been reared in their atmosphere and has insensibly become accustomed to expect the results accruing from them. Although he may devoutly believe that America lives at too high a tension, that her people demand too high a standard of comfort and efficiency, that too much emphasis is set on externals in everything from office buildings to shop windows and the objects they display, nevertheless, the comfortable consequences of this life and these standards have made their inroads upon him. When he waits five minutes longer than necessary for change in an unattractive, badly arranged shop, his vexed mind hurries to Fifth Avenue where something in the very tone of the shop windows suggests the liveliness, the smartness, the vivacity of American demand and supply. Even the best windows on Bond Street, he says to himself with some degree of truth, are dowdy compared to those which his homesick memory reviews. The smile and the courteous "Good afternoon", which invariably conclude his shopping encounters, do not tend to mollify or assuage him.

Alas! his more indirect methods of procuring what he wants fare no better. He expects (at least he expects early in this pleasurable game) that when his trousers need pressing, they will be pressed well and quickly; that when dry cleaning is imperative, it will be perfectly accomplished in a short space of time; that when he gives his orders for immediate delivery to the grocer, the chemist, or the tailor, these men will jump to execute them. When his trousers, pressed badly according to his meticulous standards, are returned to him in a week's time, when his suit is sent to Scotland to await its long deferred turn, and when no one jumps to execute his orders, he is at first amazed and then annoyed. If he stays long enough in England, his amazement and annoyance may move through the various stages of resignation to the easier state of amusement. And if he perseveres to the end, there is a chance that he may become partially converted to this incredible manner of living.

As in the matter of the telephone, his temper is surely tried by the politeness always attending the promise of delay.

"We are extremely sorry, sir, but no one works on Good Friday, we close at noon on Saturdays, Easter Monday is a Bank Holiday, and Wednesday is early closing. It will be quite impossible for us to do anything for you before Thursday week, and then, of course, we shall require several days to fulfil your order."

Nor is this courtesy always confined to the verbal.

Certain firms in England have a way of enclosing carefully worded communications when they send you your purchase or return to you the articles which they have been washing, cleaning, pressing, or repairing. From a dry cleaning firm I have several times received the following, its printed form suggesting the fact that it is often, if not regularly, sent:

Dear Madam:
We regret exceedingly that the expert methods of cleaning always employed by us have not been entirely successful in removing all the spots from the garments entrusted to our attention. We assure you of our utmost care in executing your valued orders; we hope for your continued patronage; and we beg to remain
                          Respectfully yours. . . .

When such a missive as this arrives, together with your best gown in much the same state as when it left your side two weeks ago, what are you to do? If you are wise, you will stretch out your cold feet before your cheerful English fire, ring the bell for tea—and do nothing, simply because there is nothing to do.

V

These are, on the whole, minor irritations, capable, if the weather has been decent for a brief season and if one's humour has not gone irretrievably to sleep, of being transcended into amusement. What is sometimes more difficult of transmutation are the prevailing misconceptions among the English of things across the Atlantic, or to use their own term, especially popular in Oxford and Cambridge, of *"trans-Atlantic"* life. These misconceptions (or absence of any conceptions at all) have to do with geography, topography, ethnography, and sociology.

A year ago in crossing from New York to Southampton a most charming Englishman, who had been on a brief business trip to Canada and the United States, invited me quite on his own volition to a contest. I was to write all the counties of England which I knew, and he as many as he could of the forty-eight states of the Union. Since I have spent much time in England and since my business is the teaching of English literature, I necessarily know that Cumberland is in the Lake region, that Stratford-on-Avon is in Warwickshire, and that Yorkshire does not protrude into the English Channel. My list of thirty out of the thirty-nine English counties was somewhat less than might have been expected of me. Since he had never been before in any part of the United States and since his mission while there had had to do with New York business blocks, it may be that his performance was explainable if not excusable. His list of nine out of forty-eight was as follows:

1. Vermont (which he pronounced with a French accent)
2. Susquehanna
3. California
4. Philadelphia
5. Ohigho
6. New York
7. Tex-ass
8. Virginia
9. Chesapeake

The compliments which he proffered me upon what he termed my "extraordinary feat" were, however, diminished in their effect by his tacit assumption that whereas naturally every one would wish and need to know England, there was no reason either valuable or valid why an Englishman should know the United States!

The American sojourner becomes accustomed at English social gatherings to remarks and questions such as the following:

"Is there a town in America called Denver?"

"Harvard College is in the East, isn't it, and Yale in the West?"

"You must have large rivers, then, to have all these floods."

"When you say New England, just what do you mean?"

Granted always that there may be less to draw the intelligent Englishman to America than there is to draw the intelligent American to England, granted that American political and economic life has less connection than European with the British Isles, and that American letters, at least in the past, have had relatively small relation to or interest for the English—granting all these things, or perhaps more accurately *assuming* them, the situation, reasonable though it may be, is none the less exasperating to the loyal American.

Certain Oxford and Cambridge lecturers have an annoying way of easily dispensing with much American scholarship. Their favourite adjective, *trans-Atlantic*, stands them here in good stead:

"Professor ——'s book, although it has its points, is for obvious reasons held in higher regard across the Atlantic than here."

"This article, which you might glance at if you

40

find time, is interesting like all *trans-Atlantic* ideas, but it is not to be taken too seriously."

"This book is purely *trans-Atlantic,* so take it *cum grano salis.*"

Exceptions, reassuring to the American, are always found among the English who have, for one reason or another, business, travel, or study, spent some time in the United States. These men and women are uniformly enthusiastic (in so far as the English are ever openly enthusiastic) about us and our odd ways. They may have found our business methods too zealous, too quickly effectual, our travel too hectic, our education at once far too widespread and too seriously undertaken; but they think our cities and our country beautiful, our food exciting and delicious, our eagerness engrossing, if a bit pathetic. They, at least, understand that nine-tenths of the American population is not made up of Negroes, Jews, Mongolians, and a polyglot of the riff-raff of Southern Europe; they know that kidnappers do not stand under every tenth lamp-post with furtive eyes out for perambulators, and that one can walk unarmed to the opera and the Art Institute in Chicago. They have seen the sky-scrapers rising in sunlight beyond the mist and smoke of the Hudson and in that instant have understood that one form of our architecture may be an expression of ourselves and not just a practical method of saving space. They like us, and in an outburst of unusual candour, gained perhaps from their visit to our shores, sometimes actually *say* so. And most comforting of all, like oil in our weary ears, are the new terms they occasionally find with which to characterize us. For to the American living in England nothing becomes more wearing than to be told and retold by both press and people that without doubt the United States of America is of all nations the *kindest* and *most hospitable* in the world!

III

*English Manners, Urban
and Rural*

I

AMONG all countries of the world the United States probably bears the distinction, or at least the contrast, of being relatively codeless in regard to the manners, the outward behaviour of her people. This statement does not for a moment intend the suggestion that Americans (to use the term habitually applied abroad to the residents of the "States") are an ill-mannered or a mannerless people. It simply means that at home more than elsewhere there are, in general, fewer prescribed rules of conduct, less forms and conventions, fewer things that one "does" or "does not do". This fact doubtless lies in a number of causes: the comparative youth of our country; the pioneer nature of much of its earlier life which, in place of traditional forms of behaviour, encouraged from the start widespread friendliness and hospitality; the absence from the beginning of a so-called "aristocratic ideal"; the initial insistence upon freedom and equality for all. These things have resulted in a certain sort of behaviour, easy, natural, generally acceptable, and yet not infrequently misunderstood by older countries like England where "naturalness" has been more carefully bred, more closely supervised, through centuries of insistence upon custom and usage.

In England behaviour in general is indissolubly connected with custom and usage. The English admire naturalness, but with them to be natural is, of course, to be English, which in its turn means to be the product of centuries of unwritten social precepts. The wider, more unrestrained naturalness of the American often strikes the Englishman as rude. It is not, he thinks, held within bounds as it should be. American cordiality and friendliness sometimes seem to him intrusive, are wrongly interpreted as overfamiliarity. Conversely, English repression and reserve seem at times rude to the American. Neither, strictly speaking, is rude at all, once one realizes that each is the product of the respective background of each people.

The English code of conduct abjures personal questions of all sorts, even though they may be asked with that eager interest typically American. As a matter of fact, the Englishman is not given to questions of any kind. If they do not imply intrusion into business which has nothing to do with him, they are likely either to suggest his ignorance or to make him unduly conspicuous. To be overly conspicuous in any way in England is to have bad manners. Hence the American tourist who is given to asking innumerable questions is looked upon with suspicion, sometimes with dislike, and often with a kind of superior disdain.

The English do not, for example, like to ask directions in a foreign city. They would rather blunder along for any length of time than to ask their way, simply because to do so would, first, mark them as foreigners ignorant of the country, and, secondly, would set them apart for special notice, both situations unpleasant in themselves. I have walked the streets of Paris in a state approaching starvation with an English woman, who, although she speaks excellent French, could not bring herself to ask the way to a certain restaurant! The English do not like guide-books perceptibly exposed to view; and the American reading such a volume as he gazes at a cathedral front or wanders about the Oxford or Cambridge colleges is a distasteful as well as a humourous figure to them.

The average Englishman does not look up the

pronunciation of words in a dictionary as is the
common custom in America. He may consult the
dictionary when necessary for their meaning, but
for their sound and use he relies implicitly upon
what is prescribed by custom, in other words, upon
what is said or not said. Similarly, there are certain
words absolutely taboo in this island because of their
personal, not to say intimate connotations. And the
Englishman, at least in his cursory conversation
with people at large, is rarely personal and never
intimate. For example, one does not utter carelessly
and simply, as one does at home, the word *stomach*
in England. It and, in fact, all words pertaining to
digestive functions are ruled out by English manners. Once in ignorance I used this forbidden word
openly at a tea-party, whereat the atmosphere fell to
such a degree that on the following day an explanation and apology were tendered to my hostess by the
embarrassed friend whom I was visiting! The term
sick in England implies quite accurately and sufficiently all sad ramifications having to do with the
organ in question. Nor does one thoughtlessly im-
peril his social standing by the naïve bandying
about of such a word as *bug*. This substantive,
which in America draws a wide and inclusive circle
about all insect life, connotes but one creature in

England and is ruled out, again, of course, on the score of undue intimacy. (Even as I write these words I am acutely conscious of the distressing, even disastrous mental and physical effects they may engender in possible English readers!)

Minor instances such as these only bear evidence that the English code of behaviour is all-inclusive. It is, in fact, only an old and long extension throughout the country at large of that aristocratic ideal which has made England the country of unwritten laws and which has, perhaps curiously, become the ideal of the great mass of English people. That innate respect which every true Englishman feels for himself makes him respect his neighbours as well. Their business, their weaknesses, their decisions are no concern of his; and he is distinctly tolerant of all others so long as the prescribed conventions in matters of behaviour are preserved. Manners may be external, but it is significant that in England one's relations with all, except those within one's most intimate circles, possess an externality lacking in most other countries. And it is this externality, this outward appearance, which counts so heavily among the English.

English manners everywhere are bound up with English character. Character may determine a man's exterior; nevertheless, in England at least, his exterior has an effect upon his character. The ancient motto of New College, Oxford, *Manners makyth man*, is a motto superlatively English. In England all training in behaviour begins seemingly with the ideal of Repression. It is binding upon a gentleman never to lose his self-control, at least in public, to preserve at all costs the appearance of equanimity, and the reality is likely to follow. Whether in sport or in business, in politics, at home and abroad, composure at all costs is to be sought after; and neither victory nor defeat, neither good luck nor bad, must disturb it. Above all things, don't give yourself away, say the English. This watchword has surely made of English sportsmanship the envy of the world at large, just as this ideal stamped the spirit of the English trenches in the World War. And although such a precept results also in the English suspicion of excessive amiability and a dislike of all forms of exaggerated courtesy, it is surely responsible for the good manners prevalent everywhere in town and country.

II

Even upon brief acquaintance English behaviour is apt to strike the beholder as almost automatic, almost incapable of deviation, in a word, prescribed to the *nth* degree. The English automatically keep their places in a queue and are filled with disgust at the unwonted spectacle of anyone presuming to move a step ahead of his rightful place; they never shout in public or use abusive language; they never forget their *please* and *thank you,* their *Good-morning* or *Good-afternoon* at the close of a business or social encounter; they are uniformly courteous to servants and subordinates; their *How-do-you-do?,* which automatically follows introductions to strangers, is briefly and decently said; if they shake hands, a gesture far more rare in England than at home, they do it summarily and correctly, although without undue enthusiasm. Certain American courtesies such as seating women at table or removing one's hat in an elevator are not indulged in in England. They have never been done and would doubtless strike the English as self-conscious and unnecessary.

In an English crowd or upon a London street one does not push or needlessly intrude upon one's neighbour; in trains one defers to the other occupants of the carriage before raising or lowering the window. The uniform and universal politeness in town and city shops tacitly demands of the tourist an overhauling of his own manners. There are few more courteous persons on this earth than English policemen.

If, indeed, there are any places in England where manners seem less prescribed, more free than elsewhere, the university towns of Oxford and Cambridge bear this distinction. Undergraduate life in England as elsewhere makes for extreme freedom in outward behaviour; and perhaps there is still truth in the words of Sir Harry Wildair in Farquhar's play, "I am privileged to be very impertinent, being an Oxonian." As individuals, English undergraduates are courteous; in the mass they are inclined to give the disagreeable impression of complete possession of their respective towns. In certain English dons there is sometimes evident the complacency of the over-learned, since extensive or intensive knowledge of one sort or another frequently dulls a crammed and cramped brain to outward accessories. It is but fair to say, however, that such complacency is as distasteful to the average Englishman as to the foreigner. For in itself it would imply the over-estimation of one's own importance, too great concern with one's ego, as well as too consuming a passion for the merely intellectual, all objects of ridicule in England. The rank and file of the nation would unquestionably uphold the maxim of Lord

Chesterfield, "Manners must adorn knowledge, and smooth its way through the world." There are surely no people more alive to the weaknesses of their own countrymen than are the English, and no country in which pretence and pomposity in any form is more thoroughly laughed out of court.

Terminology bears an interesting place in the manners of the English. This is but natural, since custom and prescription have had their part in proper speech to be made on proper occasions. English voices are consistently better pitched than those in America; the language even among the lower classes is more grammatically spoken; and there is a certain dignity of utterance which is not, at least generally, apparent at home. This dignity and precision, however, sometimes strike the American as humourous and not infrequently act as a damper upon his own greater ease, or carelessness, in expression.

Recently I experienced this unintentional rebuke in a London shop when I presented a cigarette lighter for necessary repair.

"Good-morning, madam," said the man about to serve me, with the usual bow. "What can I do for you this morning?"

"This thing doesn't work," said I, thoughtlessly

enough, and without any of the preliminaries which he seemed to think fitting to the occasion.

Taking the lighter from my hand and requesting me politely to take a chair by the counter, he slowly and critically began his examination, treating even the lighter with extreme respect since it was the possession of another.

"I fear, madam," he said after a few moments, "that the flint has perished. Yes," after a few moments more, "it has *utterly* perished."

I felt more uncomfortable than I could have felt had I wrongly addressed a member of the Royal Family. I rose feebly to his high station.

"Could you possibly renovate it?" I asked. "Remedy the defect?"

"Certainly, madam," said he. "If I may but detain you for a few minutes, I shall be delighted to put it in proper condition. Can I offer you the morning paper?"

Only yesterday, holes in my stockings prompting action, I went into a draper's shop,

"I want a darning-ball, please," I said to the saleslady.

She, obviously unfamiliar with my name for such an object, began to spread before me multifarious balls of wool.

"I don't mean wool," I said with some annoyance. "I mean something you place in the heels and toes of your stockings to darn them over."

"Oh," said she, "I beg your pardon. I suspect, madam, that you refer to a darning-*egg*."

"Is that what you call them?" I said. "I think that's what I want."

She rummaged in several drawers before she again turned to me.

"I'm sorry, madam," she said. "We are temporarily out of darning-eggs. I wonder if a darning-*mushroom* would serve your purpose equally as well?"

III

Manners throughout the English countryside savour of those in town and city, although they are somewhat less formal as is always characteristic of people who live on the land. Nevertheless, the same high standard of outward behaviour prevails. That respect for custom and usage which has stamped the higher circles of English life is evident also in the rural districts and among the labouring classes. There is evident as well a similar respect, quite divorced from subservience, for the upper ranks of

society in so far as they deserve to be respected, the
so-called gentry, the titled persons, the Court, and,
above all others, for the Royal Family. Whether the
English countryman is consciously aiming to imitate
his betters in his own manners and bearing or
whether he is quite unconsciously subscribing to a
traditional aristocratic ideal of behaviour can hardly
be ascertained. There is probably something of
each, plus his own self-respect as an Englishman, in
his decent and seemly conduct upon all occasions.

Much of the pleasure in my life for two years in
an English village resides in this prevalent courtesy.
That respect for the rights of others is as common in
the country as in Mayfair or Belgrave Square. It is
part of the Englishman's code, here as well as in the
town, not to intrude upon his neighbours and their
ways of doing things. They have their lives to live in
their own way, and he has his.

The English labourers and tradesmen have respect also for their work whatever it is. In this I
believe there are fewer exceptions in England than
elsewhere. They take their time at their work, do
not betray over-seriousness or too much zeal about
it, but they perform it well and take an obvious
pleasure in it, which in turn provides pleasure for
those whom they serve. The telegraph boy, who

pedals two miles from town with messages for me, tells me he enjoys his ride through the country; my gardener works on Wednesdays from dawn till dark with never a pause except to eat his luncheon and to light his pipe, seemingly satisfied and content with his seven shillings a day; I am sure of the smile and bared head of the coal man at my back door, of the milkman, and of the baker's boy.

Once last winter in a village in Hampshire the clasp of my watch-ribbon refused to function. I took it to the boot repairer, who after half a minute's work with one of his tools set it right. I asked him what I owed him and was somewhat surprised to be told that the cost was sixpence. He apparently was conscious of my surprise, for, as he took my sixpence, he said with a fine straightening of his head and shoulders:

"It's not the time, madam, it's not the work. It's the fact that *I* know *how* to do it."

In spite of the reserve characteristic of the English, people in the country seldom fail to greet one on village streets, in the fields or lanes, and to follow this greeting with some comment on the weather at hand. The usual "Good-night" used throughout England after sundown is a pleasant feature of evening walks everywhere. On the buses, which now run practically in all directions, connecting the most outlying hamlets with the nearest market towns, one customarily falls into conversation with one's neighbour in the same seat and is always rewarded with a cordiality which, although it never exceeds bounds, is never withheld and always genuine.

English country and village children are the best mannered in the western world. One simply never detects the slightest sign of rudeness among them, and for any of them to shout after a passing car, to beg, or to make personal remarks of any sort to strangers is utterly unheard-of. Whether they are taught in the elementary schools or whether they merely are nourished in the general atmosphere of politeness about them, they rarely forget to touch their caps or to bow to older people, and questions asked of them are always courteously answered with *sir* or *madam*. When they appear at one's door on Guy Fawkes Day in November with their effigies often cleverly dressed and arranged in their carts, their good manners elicit willing pennies for their fireworks; and on May Day one gladly gives to the village May Queen and her gorgeously arrayed attendants. At Christmas time boys sing carols from house to house, often in small groups of their own making, and their behaviour when they are asked indoors for sweets and pennies leaves nothing to be desired.

All in all, the manners of this England, in banks and shops, in garages and at filling-stations, in country cottages and city hotels, on London thoroughfares and in rural lanes can hardly be surpassed or even equalled. If they arise fundamentally from the English idea and ideal of Repression of the Ego at all costs, one is inclined to regard such repression as an asset and not as a liability. The grateful pleasure of the traveller and the sojourner may well offset the anxiety of the psychologist!

IV

English Trees

I

I AM in Southern France as I write these words in praise of the trees of England. Here in the bright sunlight and warm, luminous April air of Provence, with the Mediterranean before and the gaunt, tree-less spurs of the Maritime Alps behind, I look from my window upon the silvery green of olive trees growing above the ancient walls which give them security upon the hills. I look, too, upon the black green of cypresses, standing tall and straight, singly or in dense groups against the crumbling walls of wayside shrines and chapels, marking the gardens and terraces of villas, shadowing the enclosures of village cemeteries. Provence has a classic age which England lacks. Roman life is largely lost to England, in spite of the outlines of Roman roads, the survival of baths, of camps, an occasional bit of ancient city wall like that in St. Alphage's Churchyard, London, and the longer reaches of the northern wall between the Tyne and the Solway. Here it is still present. These cypresses, one easily thinks, have sprung from a long line once sheltering Roman villas upon these very slopes; the great-grandfathers of these olives supplied Roman gentlemen like Petronius and Pliny with provincial oil for their anointing.

English trees give rise to no such long reveries. In her appearance England is old, but not ancient like this smiling, sunswept land of Roman France. Even her oldest trees, the oaks in Windsor Great Park, the almost incredible beeches at Burnham, the yews spreading wide over many a quiet churchyard, do not carry one's thought beyond the Middle Ages when, through the mixture of Celt and Saxon and Norman, she was already England. To one who has studied her trees, seeing in them the pervading influences of soil and climate, there is something uniquely, almost humourously English about them. They, too, share in that mingling of qualities, that synthesis of elements, which has resulted in the singular people of England.

Not for England the long avenue of trees so characteristic of France. I remember a double row of plane trees, exactly five miles in length, shadowing a road between the French towns of Cahors and Toulouse in the province of Guyenne—trees which are in themselves worth an ocean crossing to see. There are countless other such beautiful rows of planes or Lombardy poplars, elms or chestnuts between which stretch the long French roads. Such a plan as this does not please the English. It is too self-conscious, too thought-out. There are certain new or improved highways running from London to the county towns along which trees thus arranged have been planted. Already they look out of place in England, lifeless, ill at ease, uncomfortable at being asked to stand each in exact distance from its neighbour, each expected to grow like the one next in line. They are not at home, and they show it. They may grow there, but they will never be English trees in the true sense of the word. And even where along the avenues and drives leading to great English estates beeches or limes have been planted, they have been given ample room, so that each stands in reality alone, no branches closely interlocking, no friendly intercourse one with another.

The best and noblest specimens of English trees stand in green fields or on open hillsides, singly or in small isolated groups like that on St. Catherine's hill, Winchester, with room enough among them to enable each to develop freely on its own lines. To the foreigner walking as he learns to walk, not along the roads but rather along the paths which intersect the fields everywhere, this quality of English trees is the first to impress itself upon him. Mounting the wooden stiles which, spanning the hedgerows, afford admittance to yet other fields and slopes, he looks across undulating meadows, up hills and down into small valleys, and notes how each tree stands by itself, that oak or elm, that beech or chestnut. Each is an individual, living its own life, careless of its neighbours, which never are close enough for annoyance. The green fields encircle each, dotted with grazing cattle and horses. Each receives its own share of rain and rare sunlight; each can bend to this wind and that without endangering its symmetry; each has room at sundown for the vast shadow of its own boughs and leaves.

And yet with all the freedom of wide areas about them English trees are surprisingly compact in themselves. The English elm, one of the most beautiful of trees, is not the widespread, arching variety common to New England village greens and streets. It is, instead, a closely knit tree with smaller, darker foliage and massive, thick-set branches. On a sunny April morning before its leaves have come, its green-gold flowers are like the clear glow of an English sunset after a day of rain. Similarly the branches of the oaks with their profusion of small, thick leaves are held within strict bounds, so that one seeing them has the impression of solidity and mass rather than of height and width. The black boughs of the horse-chestnuts, even with the most ample space for spreading, encircle the stout trunk in close and perfect symmetry, and so straight are held their pyramids of blossoms that they are rightly given the lovely name of Whitsun-candles. This tendency to compactness and compression is seen also in the holly, whose glossy leaves and branches spread upward and outward in a perfect cone and whose brilliant berries mass themselves in close clusters of red. The various hawthorns knit themselves closely together whether in hedgerows or in single trees, so that when England from late April till early June is red and white with "May-bloom", the impression is of dense masses of compact, starlike blossoms. A flowering lime, the most fragrant of English trees, is like a mammoth, perfectly arranged bouquet; and the continuous hum of the bees on an early summer day only serves to increase the symmetry by filling and enclosing it with a resonant monotony of sound. Even the yew, whose widespreading shade has been sung by the poets, escapes all impression of prodigality by the tremendous size of its trunk and lower branches which lend proportion to the whole.

Seeing these things, one's imagination leaps to the understanding of the likeness between English trees and English people. In both, this passion for liberty, freedom, and individualism is inextricably connected with the seemingly opposite inclination toward repression, limitation, reserve, living within bounds, the cultivation of seemliness, good manners, if you will. The first is Saxon, the predilection for sturdy independence, complacent individualism, simplicity at all costs; the second is the heritage from the Norman, the predilection for superiority, self-sufficiency, nobility in bearing, subservience to tradition, in a word, aristocracy. To the English mind liberty and freedom are indispensable, and yet they are only possible through strict adherence to certain laws within and without oneself; and it is by the very imposition of these laws by oneself that liberty and freedom are to be obtained. In this way internal freedom is naturally reconciled with external restrictions of one's own; and it is precisely in this way that the inward and the outward man forever stand in England in reciprocal relation and fellowship.

Perhaps, too, there is something of the half-forgotten Celt, whose stamp survived in part long after the Romans had withdrawn their legions, in trees as well as in people. Not for the English the fanaticism, poetry, and superstition of their Celtic neighbours, the Irish, the Welsh, and the Highland Scot; yet because there is still a bit of the Celt deep within him, the Englishman is by no means the prosaic, unimaginative, matter-of-fact being which so many think him to be. His ruling passion, love of the countryside and all that it means, goes far to disprove this conception. Cardinal Newman saw in the olive trees about Athens qualities to provoke a religious veneration. Toward the oak, forever sacred to the Celt, the Englishman yet feels something of this deep-rooted sentiment. His solid roof-trees and doors, the beams of his low ceiling, the blackened frame of his fireplace are at their best if they are made of good English oak. Toward all these things he cherishes a feeling surely akin to veneration; for second only to his passion for the land is his ideal of home. English poets sing of the oak. To Spenser in *The Shepheardes Calender* it is king of the field; to Keats in *Hyperion* its branches are charmed by the stars; and from the balladists onward the proudest boast of all is that English hearts are those of oak. Certain oaks are still set apart for honour, that of William Rufus in the New Forest, that of Robin Hood in Sherwood; and in the West Country there lingers a superstition concerning the removal of the mistletoe from its branches. It may be taken, but carefully, without injury to the sacred tree.

In such ways the trees of England are like her people, by chance or by unfathomable design. They stand about in parks and fields and rare spaces of woodland, each a law unto itself, none effacing nor for a moment forgetting that law. The wealth of room in which to grow and flourish is not incompatible with the decent curbing of one's growth and self-expression. This likeness lends to English fields and hills a kind of inevitable naturalness which no other country known to me possesses.

Some innate sense of this fellowship is surely proved by the manner in which the English are forever talking about their trees, singling out this and that for especial approbation as they walk through the fields, deploring the depredations of the too tenacious ivy, regretting the death of the oldest among them. In this they share the wisdom and understanding of King Solomon, who, when he had received both from God together with "largeness of heart, even as the sand that is on the seashore, spake of trees, from the cedar that is in Lebanon even unto the hyssop that springeth out of the wall."

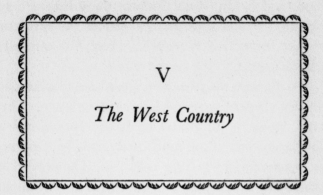

V

The West Country

I

THE two sections of England most often differenti-
ated are those large districts which go familiarly by
the names of the West Country and the North. More
or less loosely defined in boundary, they are nevertheless, I think, more characteristic in themselves of
different attitudes of mind, speech, and behaviour
than are any other sections, just as they are different
in the nature of the country which each embraces.
Because of this they offer, when studied in contrast,
a larger understanding of England as a whole and,
therefore, deserve each a chapter by itself.

So far as I know, the West Country has no definite
or accurate lines drawn about it. It is not England's
way to be definite and accurate about such things.
The counties thus loosely held together by this in-
viting name are those which look out upon the Bristol Channel on the north and face beyond their
heaths and moors the English Channel on the south

73

—Somerset, Devon, and Cornwall. To them are added Dorset, which has no northern coastline, and Wiltshire, which has no coastline at all. It is this green and pleasant land to which Hardy in his novels has recalled the ancient name of Wessex; and although he frequently portrays it in a darker hue than it presents to the less profound observer, no one has depicted it so clearly or so well.

It is, in fact, almost a country by itself, so sequestered is it in its peninsular formation from the rest of England. It is sequestered, too, in its physical character, a land for the most part of small valleys cut by small, slow rivers or by rushing trout streams —valleys enclosed either by the great moors and hills of Devon and Cornwall and by the high downs of Wiltshire or by the undulating slopes of Somerset and Dorset. And it forever gives the impression of greater seclusion than the rest of England affords by the relative smallness and completeness within themselves of its towns and its villages, between which the moors rise or the heaths and fields stretch in solitude. Plymouth in the south and Bristol in the north are its only large cities; Bath and Exeter its only sizable towns, both of which seem half asleep in the memory of a long past.

Perhaps this indelible impression of self-complete-

ness is deepened by the fact that the West Country
is pre-eminently a land of farms and fishing-villages
where self-sufficient people live from soil and sea.
This, of course, could be said of much of Norfolk,
Suffolk, and Essex or of Kent; and yet the larger,
flatter farms of East Anglia, stretching toward a far
horizon, do not suggest the detachment of those in
the west, nor are their harbours so small or so shut
in by cliffs as those of Cornwall and Devon. As to
Kent, beautiful as it is, the yearly bustle in its orchards and hop-fields, where pickers from all over
England congregate, and the long stretches of its
unsurpassed roads lend to it a more cosmopolitan
and thriving appearance than is possessed or desired
by the shires in the west.

The West Country seems, indeed, a place apart,
older than the rest of England, more deeply rooted
in her past, more jealous and tenacious of her traditions. Even its agricultural life seems more deeply
imbedded in its red and warm brown soil than it
can be in the long farmlands of the east. Its ciders
and its cheeses smack of home industries in spite of
the fact that it has its factories for them. Its sheep,
grazing by thousands on the Wiltshire downs, suggest Hardy's ancient, church-like sheep-barn where
Gabriel Oak and his labourers with patriarchal

names sheared their flocks in the spring. Its cattle in the meadows of Dorset and the green Somerset fields look more settled than elsewhere in England; and the ponies, still ranging on Exmoor and Dartmoor, seem as much a part of the land as the stags which occasionally leap through the heather.

This same seclusion and tenacious contentment is true also of its fishing-villages, which for centuries have clustered about the small, stoutly-girt harbours of Cornwall and Devon. Cadgwith, Polperro, Boscastle, and dozens like them face the Atlantic from the tiniest of coves backed by dark, precipitous cliffs. Their men fish by hand-lines and occasional trawls, live a hard and precarious life, and make small profits, retaining still in their tackle, boats, and engines much of the communal ownership of older civilizations. Their white-washed cottages perched on the cliffside are covered with flowers; their sons go into the fishing as soon as the rule of the elementary school allows; they know even today little of anything or anywhere beyond their work and the sea about them; yet by their very limitation of what is called experience, they contribute to the character of their locality.

Much of the West Country still retains traces of its Celtic origin. This is seen particularly in Corn-

wall in the dark hair, eyes, and complexions of many
of its inhabitants, and also in South and West Devonshire although to a less marked degree. It is seen,
too, in the prevalent folk-lore and in the manifold
superstitions of the simpler people, and perhaps ac-
counts to some extent at least for that reverence of
custom and tradition which is surely even stronger
in the West Country than elsewhere in England.
The past in the West Country is longer and older
than elsewhere, extending far beyond history into
the dim reaches of myth and legend. King Alfred
baked and burned the cakes in Somerset; but Ar-
thur was before him in Cornwall and, for that matter, in Somerset as well. The Romans were at Ames-
bury and on the Wiltshire downs; but Stonehenge
puzzled even their legions by its solitary eloquence
on Salisbury Plain. Joseph of Arimathea brought
the Holy Grail to Glastonbury, and from his staff
sprang the sacred thorn.

One should re-read the *Iliad* and the *Odyssey* in
Cornwall, for Cornwall is curiously Homeric. The
Greeks who traded there for ten centuries before
the Christian era must have felt pleasantly at home,
for its cliffs and headlands resemble those of the
Aegean islands, Patmos and Samos, Rhodes and San-
torin. Odysseus' descriptions of his places of reluc-

tant sojourn might fit many a Cornish harbour; and Andrew Lang's western beach with its surge and thunder was surely meant for any one of the rocky shores from Boscastle to Land's End. Even the Cornish cows, climbing the steep lanes homeward at nightfall, satisfy the repeated Homeric description with their "trailing feet and shambling gait". Small wonder that Hardy remembered Greek dramas and found tragedies "truly Sophoclean" in even the byways of this quiet country.

Small wonder, too, that he found throughout these few hundreds of miles every variety of mood and atmosphere in the land itself. There are few lonelier places in the world than the bare, windswept Wiltshire downs at nightfall, than the stretches of heath between Salisbury and Dorchester, than Bodmin Moor, than the treeless reaches of the Mendips with their black stone walls in place of hedges. There are few richer fields and meadows than the dairy lands of Somerset and Dorset, where Tess and Angel Clare milked the cows in the warm mist of summer mornings. Over all these, caught up by the sense of age which is everywhere apparent, he has thrown the shadow of Time.

Here in the West Country dialect has survived and lingers as nowhere else in England. The North has its own unique intonations, its own peculiar words as have the Midlands and the East; but in the west, especially in Somerset, grammar itself has kept much of its old usage among the country people. Pronouns are spoken without regard to cases, and verbs still defy the dictionary and good form.

"Zur", said a Somerset housemaid to her master in respect to the gardener, whom she dislikes, "Zur, I baint conzerned ower the likes o' 'ee." Which being translated reads:

"Sir, I'm not concerned over such a man as that."

To me at least there are no villages comparable to those in the west. This is a major and daring statement enough when one remembers Penshurst and Ightham in Kent, Shere, Friday Street, and Holmbury St. Mary in Surrey, Bourton-on-the-Water in the Cotswolds, the Abingtons Great and Little, Madingley, Trumpington, and Grantchester in Cambridgeshire, Sutton Courtenay and Sonning on the Thames, Little Stretton in Shropshire, and any number of others from East Anglia to Wales, from Sussex to the Lowlands. Nevertheless, I believe it is based on more than a preference born of longer association. The very seclusion of the West Country, the character of most of its industry, have resulted in relatively little change from year to year in its vil-

lages; and the nature, the contours, of the land itself have afforded incomparable situations for their
perfect churches, their old inns, their plastered and
timbered houses, and their frequent country-seats of
the mighty.

Nor has there been, relatively at least, in the west
so much of that building of council houses which
threatens throughout England the destruction of her
rural charm. It is doubtless necessary for hygienic
reasons that many thatched cottages which have been
standing for centuries and harbouring during that
time manifold ills should go; but, neither to the foreigner nor to the thoughtful Englishman, does it
seem necessary that unattractive, box-like houses,
erected with as little attention to the curves of the
road as to the lines of their own roofs, should take
their places even to afford better living conditions
for labouring people. The English village has suf-
fered little from traffic, as the filling-stations are cen-
tered mostly in the towns; but its doom is certainly
not far distant unless county and parish councils
learn to respect and preserve, at least in part, the
architecture which, perhaps by happy chance, gave
to it its charm. It must be as easy and relatively as
inexpensive to build an attractive cottage from ma-
terials native to the district, in conformity to the

lines of those that have stood for centuries, as it is to erect one that is ugly and quite out of keeping with its environment. But unless that idea and ideal are soon engendered, the English countryside everywhere will have lost much of the attraction it has long held both for the fortunate inhabitants of this island and for the visitors who come to see it.

There are council houses in the west as elsewhere, but more villages here have seemingly escaped their depredations. The small valleys and winding roads of Somerset, Wiltshire, Dorset, and Devon, the great trees everywhere, lend to their villages a charm more lacking in Cornwall except for the small fishing hamlets where the sea and cliffs offer a compensating substitute. Nor does the gray Cornish stone and flint afford in appearance the warmth and contentment of plaster and timber.

I can think of a hundred West Country villages to which I want to return not once but many times: Mells with its Roman name of honey, its fine church, and a cottage where I have eaten the best seed cakes in the world; Great and Little Elm, Horningsham, proud of its near-by great house, sleepy Lullington with its Norman font and doorway and its friendly children; Maiden Bradley and Maiden Newton, Codford St. Mary and Codford St. Peter; Whately with its remnants of an old tithe barn beside its church with a leper's squint and resonant Latin in its churchyard; Mere and Gillingham below Shaftesbury with its ancient abbey of King Alfred and the unrivalled expanse of rolling country from its cliff; Bishops Canning, Batcombe in its hollow beneath its great trees; Longbridge Deveril with its wealth of flowers; Nunney with the stones of its ruined castle bright with snap-dragons, the great oaks and timbered inn of Norton St. Philip; Porlock and Ivybridge and Tolpuddle, Barrington and Leigh-on-Mendip, Witham Friary with its abbey built to expiate the murder of Becket, Hinton Charterhouse, Marston Magna, Queen Camel, Widecome-in-the-Moor, and Stinsford with the heart of Thomas Hardy beneath the yews of its churchyard. Cornish villages in great number are named for strange and unfamiliar saints, St. Tudy, St. Teath, St. Dennis, St. Petroc, St. Columb Major and St. Columb Minor, and above all others the charming St. Mawgan-in-Pydar. And although the treeless hills of Cornwall look dark and Celtic enough when one climbs them in the rain, there are always her unsurpassed cliff-girt harbours, their quays strewn with nets and tackle, her blue-jerseyed, stooped men busy with their boats below the screaming gulls, her fuchsias and gerani-

ums clambering about white cottages facing the sea
—Coverack, Boscastle, Cadgwith, Crackington Haven, Mevagissey, and Porthscatho.

The churches, too, of the West Country equal if
they do not surpass the round towers and magnificent timber roofs of those in Essex and East Anglia.
There is hardly a village without its square gray
tower, often beautiful with Perpendicular work like
that of Probus in Cornwall, Chew Magna and Huish
Episcopi in Somerset. They are always open and together with their churchyards offer a welcome half
hour's rest to the walker and the motorist. Here,
even more than elsewhere, the church is still the
center and nucleus of village life. Its passing bells
still toll for the dying and the dead, the initial
strokes of one, two, or three signifying whether a
man, a woman, or a child has died. The West Country, except for parts of Cornwall where the
Wesleyan influence is strong, is predominantly
"Church", and in this feature as well as in others
shows that reverence for tradition which harks back
to the time when Church and State were everywhere
regarded as two aspects of one divinely ordered organism. Modernism in ways of life or of thought is
not rampant in the West Country; most people are
attached to the Church and those who do not attend

its services regularly are at least baptized at its font, confirmed at its altar, married and buried from its chancel. These are decent things to do, a part of one's patriotism as well as of one's religion. Nonconformity, except in certain Cornish districts, is not characteristic of the West Country as it is of the North; and there is still widespread the feeling that to be "Church" is socially far more respectable than to be "chapel". The vicar of the parish instructs the children in the elementary schools, still largely of Church origin and nurture; and stray nonconformist parents who do not wish Church training for their children in schools partly under the control of municipal councils may keep them at home if they desire until the weekly instruction in religion is over.

Similarly and naturally enough the West Country is more conservative in its politics than is the North. These hills and valleys, this life on the land or from the sea, do not encourage radical thought as do the mines and the mills of the North; and Squire Western's opinion of his sister, which he so vociferously voiced in *Tom Jones,* is not entirely outdated even now in most sections. Nowhere in England is the Royal Family more revered and honoured with that loyalty which at the time of the

Jacobite Rebellion aroused thousands of West Country men to offer their services for King and Country. The village home or the village inn which does not bear upon its walls pictures of the King and Queen, the royal princesses, the royal dukes and duchesses is the exception.

"They are not just the King and Queen," said a Somerset farmer to me a year ago. "They are the heads of our own families, and they are examples to us all in all good things."

The fine and lovely homes of the nobility, which are common throughout these five counties, arouse interest and admiration in most West Country people. Since to own land and to build one's house upon it is the consuming passion of most Englishmen everywhere, the ownership of land is looked upon with respect and good-natured envy; and it is safe to say that there is less prejudice and ill-will here than elsewhere toward the amount owned and the use made of it. I have heard again and again from all sorts of people the expression of genuine regret and sadness in that heavy taxes and death duties have resulted in the abandonment of so many great houses and in the necessary disposal of their lands.

Thus the West Country. A sunnier land than

much of England, a country of farms, orchards, and cider presses, fat cattle, cheese, and clouted cream, good ales and beer, wool and pork, hams and bacons, butter and strawberries, pilchards, mackerel, and shellfish. A land of self-respecting people, not too eager for innovations, bred to old loyalties and nurtured by them. A land which bears on its face in a score of places stone monuments and earthworks antedating the Romans by two thousand years, and much of which remained Celtic long after the rest of England became Saxon. A land which more than half believes its legends, has pride alike in its sea-kings of the past and its fishermen and sailors of the present, honours its yeomen farmers, some of whom have held their selfsame acres for centuries and lent to them their names. A land of slow speech and contented people who feel, perhaps with some truth, that they are the most English of England, and who, wherever they are, utter the name of the West Country with conscious and pardonable pride.

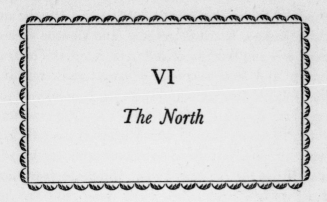

VI

The North

I

ONE approaches the North, if he is wise, by way of the high, close hills of Derbyshire, now green and sunswept, now dark, desolate, and barren like the Pennines between Bishop Auckland and Penrith. There are few districts in England lovelier than this of the Derbyshire Peak, the green fertility of certain of its hills recalling the south, the dark, clean slopes of others introducing one to the wide, high stretches of the North.

Like the West Country the North has no clearly defined boundaries. To the southerner engaged in industry it connotes the black, depressing towns of Lancashire and Yorkshire where smoke from mills and mines darkens the sunniest sky, where men speak in broader, less modulated voices than those in the south, where the more radical elements of political and economic thought are engendered by necessity and by the wilder, freer winds that sweep across wider, higher, more barren moors. To the farmers of Sussex ploughing their warm, reclaimed marsh lands and to those of Surrey and Somerset content on their sunnier slopes, it connotes, if they have travelled that far, great sweeps of high land grazed upon by muscular, windswept sheep or planted to hardy crops of oats, wheat and potatoes, fields bounded by black walls of stone instead of green hedges, walls stretching like long pencils or crawling like slow, black snakes over the wide undulations of hills and valleys. To southern shepherds it means the high fell pastures of Westmoreland and Cumberland, cut in the spring by rushing streams and in the winter swept by piercing, relentless winds.

To most dwellers in the south, in the West Country, or in the Midlands, the North has few charms. It seems somehow less English than the England which they know. Perhaps to the foreigner it seems, at first, less English also, less conservative, less old and traditional, less sure of itself, more given to new ways of thought, more likely to suggest new and untried ways of doing things, more hospitable, less cautious and correct in its readier acceptance of strangers. The southerners and West Country people whom I have known are glad they do not come from the North, excellent land that it is. They like their more closely intrenched ways of life and of thought, their cleaner, tidier, smaller towns, their ancient schools and universities, their more closely knit fields, their less hazardous industrial life. Their inheritance seems more sure and certain within them. Although they do not often say it, one gathers that they think the south more cultivated in speech and manners than the North, much as dyed-in-the-wool New Englanders think provincially that a Middle Western lineage is a bit unfortunate, much as the Virginian thanks his lucky stars that Alabama or Georgia is not, by the Grace of God, the portion meted out to *him*.

The North is, in fact, all of these things, but it is many more as well. From the southern point of view it *is* less English, less established in certain ways. But newness must be carefully defined before it can be applied to the North. To one who has tramped its most northern moors, looked southward from the grass-grown stones of its Roman wall, and followed its straight, undeviating miles of road, stretching on and on like the roads of France, it has aspects of age possessed by no other part of England. Rome is closer here than in the south. These roads suggest her masonry, these black walls her taut security. It

is easy to hear the tramp of her legions across Bowes
Moor, to see her encampments on a hundred barren
hills. Her imperators, one thinks, brought her hardi-
est soldiers northward, leaving men of lesser stature
on Salisbury Plain and by the Cambridge rivers.
The North is a land of perpetual yesterdays, and
the very vacancy of her untenanted moors goes even
beyond the Roman and the Celtic to the prehistoric.

The North has been from long forgotten times
the land of strife and the hardships which strife
engenders. Ruins of castles like that of Brougham
by its swift river suggest centuries of border warfare. Northern bishops in the Middle Ages must
perforce be fighting clerics quite as well as spiritual
props, as Durham Castle bears witness beside its
stout cathedral. And the new strife in its industrial
towns where for a century and more men have been
fighting for a decent livelihood seems but a meet
inheritance from former days.

It is true that there are few more ugly, more depressing places on this earth than the industrial
towns of northern England. Their very names lack
the euphony of the south: Manchester, Staleybury,
Leeds, Bradford, Halifax, Sheffield, Crewe, and Pres-
ton. If you wish contrast in its most stark and unre-
lieved state, compare any one of these with any one

of the southern cathedral towns: Winchester, Salisbury, Wells, or Canterbury. Cathedral towns are mellow and venerable, beautiful, content, and secluded, with a past in which one drowsily rests. A bit complacent perhaps, effete even, but satisfying. The northern towns in comparison are harsh, ugly, restless, discontented, with no past that is discernible in their bleak present. If there were once romantic doings upon their sites, fairs and travelling plays, ancient villages with their merry-makings, they are gone beyond any possibility of recall, lost in soot and grime and piles of stone. They are black towns, often under a dark sky which they hourly make darker. Rows upon rows of identical gray houses, where strident women with untidy babies stand in doorways and under-nourished children crowd the pavements; smells of cheap petrol, fish and chips, smoke and wet woollen; treeless streets; advertisements for Lyons' tea, Capstan and Woodbine cigarettes; miserable shops displaying through grimy, unwashed windows pink rock candy, drill overalls, tinned sardines, sticky kippers, sucking dummies for babies, garish underwear, impossible hats. Miles upon miles of iron railings and gray cobbles within the towns, and on their outskirts unsightly piles of waste from quarries, mills and mines until at last the moors rise and mercifully shut them from sight.

But life stirs in these towns whereas in contrast it slumbers in green cathedral closes and in the narrow, lovely streets of Salisbury and Wells. Strife is among them as unremitting as in the days of border warfare; hard work in mines and textile mills; women weaving and spinning while discontented men tend the families at home; the bitterness of unemployment; a fierce desire for justice; a suspicion of old ways merely because they are old.

It is but natural that the North should have different manners from those nurtured in the south or in the West Country, cruder, less polished perhaps, but genuine and hearty. The North, together with its wider lands, has more of the nature of a pioneer country where the common hardships both of town and of farm labour lend a larger friendliness to its people. The broader speech of more open northern mouths has a more welcoming accent than one finds in the south. Men and women go out of their way in cordial greeting to the stranger. The American sojourner or traveller often feels more at home in the North, for there is a bustle about northern towns and a breadth in northern country which one does not find elsewhere in England. Things here are still on the make; the unsettled future is a matter for cogitation and brisk effort.

Northern people possessed of decent livelihood are good providers. Tables groan with food: bacon pies, steak and kidney, apple pasties, shortbread, rolls and ham, pickles and cheese, trifles and cocoanut cakes, innumerable cups of hot cocoa and earthen pots of violent tea. Men walk with legs wide apart; women are larger and more buxom than in the south. People are more objective in their outlooks, possess a stronger humour since it springs from a sterner reality.

The North unlike the south and the West Country is not so wholly grounded in the Established Church. It is rather the home of Nonconformity. Wesleyans, Congregationalists, and Baptists, together with divers other lesser brands of Dissent, flourish in the manufacturing and milling towns. Their larger and more pretentious buildings are termed churches here rather than the "chapels" of the south. The universities of Manchester and Leeds, Sheffield and Durham, although they lack the prestige of Oxford and Cambridge, offer wider educational opportunities to young men and women of the working classes. They cannot place upon their graduates the social stamp of those aristocratic foundations; they do not make gentlemen in the Oxford and Cambridge sense; but they give the specialized training for which Oxford and Cambridge have neither time nor inclination. Class distinctions, though still present, are less binding, less immovable in the North. Members of industrial firms, themselves sprung from families who once spun and wove in poor homes, marry into the "County", while in turn many of the County families engage in industry.

Were not the North so largely given to manufacturing, in connotation as well as in fact, were not so great a part of its area blackened by its hideous towns, it would not seem so much less English than the south and west. It is, indeed, this very intrusion of town life which is at root responsible for the impression it gives, for the feeling which the southerner bears toward it. For the English are not, fundamentally, a town people; the very idea of town is alien to them. Unlike the people of Munich or Florence, Paris or Geneva, who live in their beautiful cities from inclination and taste, the Englishman looks upon a town merely as a place in which to earn a necessary living; and the foremost emotion which he feels for those who must live always where that living is earned is pity. Moreover, the great industrial centers of the North smack too literally of the nineteenth and twentieth centuries to be attractive to an old civilization, securely rooted in the Middle Ages, and still bearing in its busiest southern towns an eighteenth century stamp at the latest.

But once one has left the dreary wastes of the northern towns, once cranes and derricks, piles of black waste, clouds of smoke, grimy streets and sickly trees are left behind, England again asserts herself, a different England, it is true, and yet in many respects the same. The high fields of Northumberland are as open and friendly to the plough as those south and west; the Yorkshire dales are as lovely as the Devonshire valleys; the high coastline below Berwick-on-the-Tweed vies with the Cornish cliffs in beauty and romance; the rolling moors north and east of York, rising dark and fragrant above the vale of Pickering and the valley of the Esk, are as splendid as those of Somerset, and a clearer, more invigorating wind blows across them. Skies are wider and higher, clouds more varied and magnificent. There are fewer cottages in England more appealing than those of white-washed stone in Cumberland and Westmoreland with roses clambering over their symmetrical roofs.

There is a sense of larger freedom in this northern country than in that of the south. To realize this one has but to stand on any one of the dark hills beyond Bowes Moor and look southward. The land rises and falls, stretching on and on, divided by black walls, tenanted by cream-coloured, black-faced sheep. Few houses interrupt the long undulations of the soil itself. Westward rise the mountains of Cumberland and Westmoreland, blue, black, or gray as the weather commands.

It is this freedom of wind and sky, this clearness of atmosphere, this breadth of vision, which England needs to complete the definition of what she is. Her character would be immature and wanting without these great stretches of country and the sturdy, independent, thrifty people who inhabit them. The North is the yeast in the wholesome bread that is England; and even a partial understanding of that which is England and English would be unfinished and, therefore, imperfect without such towns as Manchester, without the long, tumbling reaches and the far horizons of the northern moors.

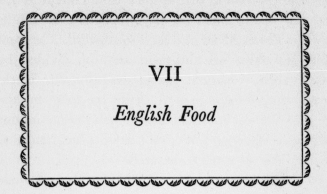

VII

English Food

I

"ONE does not come to England primarily to eat,"
wrote an American traveller of the nineteenth century. "For gustatorial elegance and enticement one
goes to France. Wanting France, the epicure would
best stay at home."

There are certainly times when the twentieth century American traveller or sojourner in England
echoes this sentiment. Whatever laudable qualities
the English may possess in their selection, preparation, and consumption of food, elegance, originality, diversity, and imagination are not among them.
Even in those massive banquets of the seventeenth
century, chronicled by Pepys, or in the gustatory
achievements of Dr. Johnson there is little of the
Epicurean discoverable. A vast distance lies between
the terms *fully fed* and *highly fed*. The former state
is well known to the English; their temperament,

inability, and disinclination serve to keep them far removed from the latter.

There is vivacity, *finesse*, genius, even spiritual insight in the cooking and serving of food in France. I sit down to a late dinner at Annecy after a day of hard driving through a spring snowstorm in the French Alps. Following a *potage* which touches the soul as well as the stomach, *homard a l'Americaine* is ceremoniously set before me.

"Your name is wrong," I say to the waiter in bad French. "We cannot cook like this in America."

"Ah, Madame," he says to me in excellent English. "The name is but politeness. The seas about America are still too young for such lobster! And the cooks, are they not too young, also?"

Under the July plane trees before an inconsequential hotel in the Dordogne Valley hearts of *artichaux* delicately embraced by *pâté de foie gras* raise my mind to the contemplation of Ultimate Perfection. On Palm Sunday in the sunswept square of Castellane, after three hours of following the tortuous curves of the Route des Alpes, I eat *une casserole des champignons* in the buoyant company of a score of villagers and country people just returned from late Mass. The café is called *L'Auberge de Bon Accueil*. My neighbours at the orange-covered tables

eat yellow-shelled *escargots* with the slow, apprecia-
tive relish of the French at food, while Madame
bows and smiles and bustles, secure in the knowledge that she has named her house well. She brings
from her own cellar her six-franc carafes of *vin du
pays,* placing them before her guests with flourishes
which instantly transform them into clear bottles of
Montrachet or the deep red of Chambertin.

A waiter in Beauvais terminates my indecision
with outspread hands and the most complete of
bows:

"If you will allow me the courtesy, Madame, I
choose for you. I select your lunch myself. I promise you, you will be well pleased."

There is more than pleasure in his *entrecôte*
delicately hedged with fresh watercress, his *poulet,*
his *salade de pissenlits* with just a hint of the bit of
garlic with which, in his dexterous mixing of the
dressing before my fascinated eyes, he has thrice en-
circled his bowl. Something of his own pride in the
cooking of his house, in the etiquette with which
he serves me, in his interrogative "Madame?" as he
places each course before me, transcends the mere
eating of delicious food. He knows, and I begin to
see, that there is an imaginative appeal in such a
process as this. My emotions respond simultaneously

with my stomach, and a mystical understanding wavers between us as he opens the door for me to leave.

In a dark downstairs restaurant on the Rue des Saints-Pères in Paris *Monsieur le propriétaire,* himself the head waiter, escorts his guests to the door and with marked ceremony shakes hands with each. There is between us at this moment more than the cherished memory of his *jambon* cunningly caramelled with fresh pineapple. There is mutual pride in a rare achievement, mutual acknowledgment that *because* of his *jambon* Seine boats and book-stalls, the gray towers of Notre Dame possess a new meaning to us both.

I have never experienced emotions such as these in English restaurants and inns. There are others, to be sure, but they are not the same. The English are a ceremonious people, but their ceremony is not evident in the dispensing or the partaking of food. It is reserved for more obvious, less personal occasions, such as the crowning or the burial of a king, such as the opening of a University library, or the presentation of the keys of the City of London. To experience themselves or to engender in others an excess of emotion over mere food would seem to them immoderate and, as such, both unwarrantable and unseemly. For an English hotel proprietor or head waiter to behave like Monsieur in the Rue des Saints-Pères would be clearly to make an exhibition of himself, to exploit his ego, terms of reproach sedulously to be avoided. That inward satisfaction which all true Englishmen show in their eating and drinking is quite sufficient for them, without any display of externalities, which might betray superabundant feelings, always to fight shy of whenever possible. Hazlitt admirably shows that inward satisfaction when at the close of a long day's walk he speculates over his tea his probable choice of his dinner. "Eggs and a rasher, a rabbit smothered in onions, or an excellent veal cutlet."

This suspicion of superfluous emotion, of all manner of excess, is clearly evident in the Englishman at his table. He does not want his meat served up with sauces that disguise its taste, seeing in this a violation against the nature, the honest character, of what he is eating. The *jambon* of *Monsieur le propriétaire* has no attraction for *him*. He wants good Yorkshire ham with a dash of English mustard. When he eats roast beef, he wants the good, substantial beef of old England, raised on home pasturage, and he wants it to taste of itself, not of something else. Moreover, if it wants seasoning, he prefers to season it in his own way. The absence of salt and pepper on a French table is intolerable to him. Nor does he want his perennial vegetables, his omnipresent boiled potatoes, his winter cabbage, cauliflower, and brussels sprouts, his summer beans and peas, cooked in butter or swimming in cream sauce. He wants them as they *are,* sitting docilely, perhaps a bit stolidly, in the partitioned vegetable dish and waiting for any attention he may choose to give them. He has no fondness for dressed-up, flighty foods, dislikes fancy ices, intricate salads, unfamiliar sweets. He knows where he is when he is eating gooseberry tart, treacle sponge, and suet pudding; and he likes to know where he is. Garnishes, condiments, flavourings, spices, relishes, appetizers—these seem to him unnecessary and excessive, especially when they disguise his fare. The banquet which Keats prepares in *The Eve of St. Agnes* is the most un-English of menus. No true Britisher from the Middle Ages until now would touch even the fringes of it, before or after his elopement! A bit of chutney, good curry, some Worcestershire, and the ubiquitous mustard-pot do him very well. His food, which to other palates may seem somewhat solid, even heavy, is just what he wants. It connotes the well-defined, the genuine, the tangible, and authentic, in a word the *substantial,* and he likes it that way.

Nor does he care for any sort of display in its serving. Here, too, his dislike of the excessive comes in. He wants it set before him in a decent and seemly manner, not bowed in with needless ostentation. He wants his soup hot in a spacious soup plate, his roast beef and potatoes ready before him in their stark simplicity, his generous slice of bread or his buxom roll beside him with the best New Zealand butter, his stout pudding in a good, ample dish, his generous glass of ale poured out as it should be. He does not want any theatrical capers or hand-shaking from *his* waiter, who should know his business, and who, if he does, gets a sixpence; if he does not, gets nothing at all.

Convention, custom, and tradition, always held by the Englishman in deepest reverence, are present in his eating. There are certain rites here as elsewhere to be strictly observed. One eats mustard with pork, ham, bacon, sausage, beef, and sometimes with veal. To eat it with lamb or with mutton betrays the foreigner or the bohemian, both persons unfortunate from the Englishman's point of view in that they do not know or do not care for the proper ways of doing things. Red currant jelly and a reasonable supply of mint sauce are eaten with lamb and mutton, just as homemade bread-sauce is always eaten with chicken. The Englishman is annoyed by the prevalent American custom, persistent among the young, of smoking before or during a meal. He calls it bad manners and is inclined to stare when he sees it among American travellers in restaurants and hotels. Like the preacher in Ecclesiastes, he is convinced that there is a prescribed place and time for all things, and he prefers them to be kept snugly and unobtrusively within their own boundaries.

He is used to certain foods and apparently never tires of them. His tranquil and eager consumption of brussels sprouts or of cabbage on a conservative average of five days out of seven throughout the winter strikes awe and admiration in the mind of the foreigner. Here, one thinks, is proof of that unruffled tenacity which has built the British Empire! Here, one knows, is the steadiness and endurance that weathered the trenches in France! His breakfasts in particular persist in their unchanged entirety from January to January. When Izaak Walton wrote in the seventeenth century of "a good, honest, wholesome, hungry breakfast," he was aptly characterizing the average Englishman before his table at nine A.M., even though his own morning fare was of a slightly different nature. Porridge with milk, rarely with cream, fish, bacon (*or* sausage *or* liver, *or* kidneys, *or* cold ham) and eggs, toast and orange marmalade, tea or coffee, the *Times* or the *Daily Mail,* a terse comment upon the weather and then calm, good-natured silence—these are the morning features and attributes of most English homes. The Englishman favours a good breakfast, and to him much of its goodness lies in the fact that it does not vary from day to day.

When Hazlitt was deciding among bacon, rabbit, and cutlet for his dinner, he doubtless was not for a moment perturbed over the potatoes, safe in the comfortable knowledge that they would be neither fried nor baked, neither mashed nor browned—but *boiled*. There are few more obvious, natural, apparent, ostensible, plain, intelligible, literal, and downright objects on this earth than a boiled potato! Before it imagination droops and dies. Reality is for once secure and circumscribed, defiant of metaphysics. Perhaps for these reasons boiled potatoes approach in England the distinction of being the national dish.

Last fall I travelled from Euston to Liverpool, en route for Ireland. At seven P.M. I took one of those desultory journeys through the train for dinner, a journey characteristic of English trains, which leads one after a long succession of coaches through a couple of luggage vans where carrier pigeons sit in crates among trunks, eggs, cheeses, perambulators, hams, a dog or two, rose trees, shrubbery of sorts, bicycles, and sundry unidentified bundles. I found sitting opposite me at the table an Englishman in the usual tweeds drinking a glass of sherry and reading his *Evening Standard*. The dinner was in every feature what one might expect after a year's experience—pea soup, Dover sole, roast lamb, gooseberry tart. The Englishman studied the menu with some perturbation, not to say annoyance, and beckoned peremptorily to the waiter.

"About these potatoes," said he in tones of opprobrium.

"You have your choice, sir," replied the waiter. "Mashed or lyonnaise."

"I don't want either," said the gentleman simply and succinctly. "I don't like mashed, and I've never tried the other. Do you mean to say that you have no boiled potatoes?"

"I'm sorry, sir. We had them last night and the night before, but we thought as how a change might be welcome."

"I daresay," thundered the gentleman. "But I

don't like changes, nor do I see the point of them on a train. I'm used to my potatoes boiled, and that's how I like them."

"I'm sorry, sir," repeated the waiter. "I'm afraid there isn't time for boiling."

"Certainly not," said the gentleman. "*You* needn't apologize. It's the railway's fault. I never heard of such a thing!"

"Many people like the lyonnaise, sir," timidly suggested the waiter, with the politeness always common to English waiters.

"I daresay," remarked the gentleman again, returning to his *Standard*. "But I venture to think that more like them boiled. I'll take neither, thanks."

Breakfast toast in England is traditionally cold. It is cut in triangles, which, apex upward, sit in the partitions of an open toast-rack. Hot buttered toast is sometimes served for tea, but rarely, if ever, for breakfast. The English like their toast cold. Moreover, they are chary of innovations. Upon a visit to English friends in Somerset my hostess, who lives during the winter in America, suggested one morning the introduction of an electric toaster. Her father, a Tory of the Queen Anne school, received her proposal with incredulity and deep disgust.

"Make toast on the table instead of in the

kitchen?" cried he. "I never heard of such a thing! It may be done in America but not in this country. Besides, the toast would be hot, and hot toast for breakfast is very indigestible."

It is safe to say that English cooks do not enjoy, at least abroad, the reputation either of the French or of the American. Yet they do some things excellently and a few superbly. Their cooking of meats leaves little to be desired; their chickens served with sausages and bacon are memorable; their plum puddings are unsurpassed. The Yorkshire puddings which my housekeeper for two years has constructed for me rise like the turrets of some castle at sundown, crisp and golden, and with an appeal to the imagination perilously akin to that inspired by cooking across the Channel. I shall long remember the sizzling sausages served me on Sunday morning in a little restaurant, once a Friary, under the shadow of St. Benet's Church, Cambridge, sausages rivalling those at Simpson's on the Strand, that rendezvous of all who want to enjoy cooking distinctly English at its best and noblest. And as for the making of tea, at least two centuries of practice and unqualified devotion have made the English masters of the art. To boil water and pour it over tea leaves seems an operation simple enough; yet no other people approach the English in this, just as nowhere else are found in the late afternoon such crumpets, such hot buttered scones, such mellow, resilient plum cakes, freighted with cherries and raisins. An English tea in the garden of the simplest roadside cottage is an event not to be forgotten or elsewhere repeated.

It is, in fact, in the making and drinking of innumerable cups of tea that the English betray their peculiar imagination, an imagination seemingly lacking in much of their cookery. The tea hour in England approaches closely to the ritualistic both in manner and in spirit. From four to six the nation is at ease from the Channel to the Lakes; and it is safe to say that understanding, sympathy, congeniality, and harmony are brewed within countless earthen teapots upon the leaves of India or of China. Nor is tea relegated only to a given time or taken only to appease hunger and thirst. A cup of tea at any hour settles problems, eases heartaches, promotes neighbourliness, marks seasons of rejoicing over good fortune. I myself, caught up in the spirit, have arisen on a bitter winter night to boil the kettle at three A.M., confident that the cheerful sight of its black rotundity on the hob before a hastily replenished fire would set the cold, dark English world aright!

That the English on the whole show little originality and less diversity in their cooking, that their table service is adequate but not inspiring, that they stoutly eschew frills of all sorts, suspect innovations, and cling to the familiar and the tried—reasons for these things lie quite honestly and simply in the English character. Their food is like themselves, durable, established, inviolable; and no one with a grain of sense, humour, or imagination would wish it one jot or one tittle different from what it is.

VIII

Twelve Ricks

I

UPON my return to England last October, after some weeks at home, I found upon the farm land just beyond my garden hedges twelve ricks of hay and grain, placed there during the harvest. The long, flat fields, which I had seen in the spring and in the early summer change from brown and gray rain-soaked soil to the green of peas and beans, clover, grass, and wheat, bore now upon their yellowing surface these concentrated symbols of their fulfilled, completed life. The ricks were beautifully made, their brown sides true and straight, their tops carefully thatched, each bearing at the extreme end of its roof peak a jaunty tuft like a tiny, squat chimney. I had missed seeing them piled and treaded, the careful eyes of the farmer shaping them well against the coming of the thatcher, who would cord and bind their roof slopes against the rains and winds of winter; but this regret was lessened in the sudden surprise and pleasure of seeing them upon the cropped field like some ancient, silent village in their simple, grave design. As a group, huddled there beneath the pale English sky, they gave the impression of a careful study in proportion and symmetry, as though the farmer to whom they belonged had had an eye to perfection in form and placement as well as to the secure storing of his harvest; and I have been grateful to him, although he knows as little of my pleasure in his work as I of his name or of his intention.

Of all the manifold pleasures which England has afforded me during a two years' sojourn, none has surpassed that which these twelve ricks have given from October until early spring. I have gazed at them in all weathers, at all hours of daylight, and beneath the moon on still winter nights when the sky has cleared after a long day of rain. I have risen foolishly early in the morning to watch them emerge from the darkness, trying in vain at six o'clock to catch their vaguest outlines in the blackness, perceiving an hour later the blurred form of their huddled indistinctness, seeing at eight o'clock their coming clearly into shape and form beneath the milk-white sky, against the brown and green fields about and around them. Under the pale winter sunshine of noon their slowly weathering colour has been warm and clear, dull only in comparison with the red of the cattle who have found food and shelter among them. By four o'clock on January afternoons they have again faded into half light and by five into darkness. They have stood dark and silent against flaming sunsets and have caught the clear gold of November afternoon skies, their tufted chimneys the last to lose the glow. Their gigantic shadows have now merged with one another, now stretched far into the fields.

A rare wet snowstorm has plastered their roofs with white; they have stood taut and secure against Cambridgeshire winds tearing across the fens. Heavy dews and mists have lent a ghostly appearance to them, made them like some mysterious northern settlement swept by fine snow. English frosts have clothed them with half an inch of rime and held them sparkling in the sun for eight long hours of a cold, clear day.

Every night at bed-time, when I have swung wide my casement windows, I have seen or not seen them, according to the vagaries of the weather. The full moon has brought them out clearly, the half moon, in shadow. By their very presence in the rain and fog of moonless nights they have lent an odd security to sleep.

In late January and early February the threshing began. Before it was light in the morning I heard the rumble and clatter of farm wagons in the lane behind my hedgerows and, as soon as the slow dawn had made working possible, the monotonous whirr and jangle of the thresher. Now the ricks became populous with men, feeding from their roofs the great machine with their well-stored hoard. Now their symmetry was lost, their completeness destroyed, their silence ravaged by the shouts of workers and the reverberating drone of engines in motion. Smoke and flying chaff filled the air, now clear in the sunlight, now lost in the dullness of overhanging clouds.

By early April, when I returned from some weeks in France, they had quite gone. Beyond the glistening, rain-washed black-thorn of the hedges, now beginning to be starred here and there by white, there were only shreds of yellow straw on the bare, awakening fields.

Yet in the brief months of their presence the twelve ricks were not only satisfying to look at. They connoted the stability of life upon the land, the everlasting prose of labour, the nameless line of those who plough and till and harvest, the long, continuous epic of the soil. They rolled the centuries swiftly back to Vergil and Horace, Homer and Hesiod, to other sheaves and stacks gathered together on the high fields of Italy and in the valleys of Greece. In the grave designs of their simple, classic outlines they were impervious to time, bound life and labour together, knew no past or future, and lent a singular security to that round of existence which will once more at harvest place them in the field.

IX

"This Royal Throne of Kings"

I

ONE morning in the summer of 1930 while I was staying at a small hotel in Cambridge, I came downstairs for an early breakfast to find my waitress in tears. Distressed at this unexpected and yet obviously genuine sign of personal sorrow on the part of one usually given to high spirits, I ventured, when she had brought me my eggs and bacon, to inquire its cause. She gazed at me in surprise tinged with reproof that I could spread out the morning *Times* quite as usual, and said in a broken voice accompanied by more tears:

"I'm that grieved for the poor Duchess, madam. We all wanted a boy for her, and now that it's a girl, I'm sure her heart is broken."

She referred to the birth in Glamis Castle of the second daughter to the Duke and Duchess of York, and so real was her own perturbation over this pleasant event, until then unknown to me, that I felt in no small measure guilty enough as I cheerfully made my good English breakfast.

In November, 1934, upon the eve of the marriage of Princess Marina to His Royal Highness, the Duke of Kent, my cook was similarly plunged into anxiety for fear of some untoward event which should endanger any member of the Royal Family en route to Westminster Abbey for the ceremony. Meeting her upon the bus, which was bearing us both homeward in the late afternoon, I listened to the unburdening of her troubled mind as we walked together from the bus station to the house.

"You can't tell," she confided to me, "what sort of people there'll be watching that procession. That's the worry of it. There may be Roosians or Italians, or them from other queer countries—the good Lord alone knows what trash there'll be along those London streets! I shan't rest easy in me bed tonight, and I'll be that thankful when tomorrow sees it over and done."

We listened to the wedding over the wireless, the cook, the housemaid, the gardener in the drawing-room together with those of us who made up our American family in England. We drank a health in sherry to the new Duke and Duchess of Kent, all standing solemnly with meet emotion once the

Archbishop of Canterbury had pronounced his blessing upon them, and the organ was thundering out the recessional march. The cook felt immeasurably improved once it was "over and done" with no pistol shot shattering the cheers of the London throngs; and the house gradually resumed its normal tenor now that she felt at peace in her kitchen.

During that long night of last January when King George V lay dying in Sandringham, no one possessed of a wireless and a grain of imagination could have failed to be profoundly moved by that singular unity of thought, that stability and permanence of feeling, which make of the British people one family with a sovereign as its head. With the realization that the genuine emotion in our own living-room was in those hours duplicated and deepened by that in millions of others throughout the country and the British world, we listened each fifteen minutes between nine o'clock and midnight to the solemn, unvaried words of the announcer:

"The King's life is drawing peacefully toward its close."

When I went to bed in the early hours of the morning after the final news had reached us, I saw from my cottage window lights in practically every village house where, surely in common with other

villages from the Channel to the Shetlands and Ork-
neys, one people had been watching in reverence and
affection.

On the Sunday following the King's death a portion of the Burial Service from the Book of Common
Prayer was read in every church, large and small, in
England. In the beautiful church of the tiny village,
which has been my home for two years, every seat
was filled with the people of the parish, gentry and
common folk, grown-ups and children, masters and
servants, Boy Scouts, Girl Guides, the British Legion
with lowered standards before the altar. Everyone
who possessed requisite black was in full mourning,
and those who could not wear it in full wore some
symbol of it on whatever clothing they had, even to
the smallest child. The atmosphere throughout the
service was that of the funeral of one near and dear
to every person present; and I could not be surprised
by the tears on faces everywhere since they were so
perilously near my own.

The new King on the first Sunday in March spoke
to the Empire at four o'clock. I shall always remember the afternoon, cold and dark with showers of
rain and sleet, for I was driving in the West Country and anxious to reach some inn with a wireless so
that I should not miss the King's first message to his

people. At ten minutes before the hour, after hurrying over wind-driven Exmoor, we drew up before the old *Ship Inn* in the village of Porlock in Somerset, more intent to hear the King than to drink our tea. The inn graciously offered its kitchen and its poor receiving set; and here at four we gathered with the pot-boy in his leathern apron, the kitchen maid, and the waitress to listen to the address. A coal fire burned in an open grate; a cat with five kittens slept in a clothes-basket; the maid ceased her clatter of the tea things; the kettle steamed on the hob; the rain beat against the low windows—while we as the only visitors stood with the servants of the kitchen to hear the voice of King Edward VIII.

Here in a fifteenth century inn the same atmosphere prevailed as on the other occasions which I have tried to picture, now generated by three of the more humble members of English society—an atmosphere at once created and pervaded by the same deep-rooted and impregnable sentiment, the present source of which, at least, may be partly explainable in the wise words of the King himself:

"My constant care shall be to continue to promote the well-being of my fellowmen."

To those thousands of Americans, who in May of 1935 witnessed the Jubilee of the King and Queen

and in January of 1936 saw the King's body borne
through the gray streets of London on its way to
Windsor, the perception of this sentiment and the
recognition of its reality were alike inescapable.
None of us can ever forget those vast throngs of
people, many of whom had cheerfully passed the
May and the January night preceding each occasion
on the pavement in order to be assured of their
places in the morning. Nor can we ever forget the
joy of the first procession or the heavy sorrow of the
second: the quick prance, and the dull thud of
horses' feet; the seemingly endless contingents of
Life, Horse, and Coldstream Guards, Irish Fusiliers,
Scotch Pipers, Colonials, Grenadiers, Marines; the
shouts, and the dead silence; the brilliance of colour,
and the depth of black and purple; the outpouring
of joyous music, and the measured beats of the Dead
March together with the measured sound of foot-
steps through the crowded, silent streets.

II

The perception and the recognition of the impregnable reality behind these things remain; but
the understanding of it is more difficult, especially
to those of us who, not being English, must forever
be spectators rather than participators of an emotion

and an idea foreign to those in which we have been engendered and nourished. The grief of the waitress in Cambridge, the anxiety of my cook, the personal sorrow of the villagers among whom I have lived—these I know through a two years' sojourn in England to be not only real but typical of English people taken as a whole. From whence springs personal devotion such as this, asks the foreigner, a devotion united, consistent, seemingly unshakable, which terms even an Opposition as "His Majesty's most loyal" and which makes of England today as in the age of Shakespeare "this royal throne of kings"?

Assuredly it does not spring merely from the tactful and concentrated efforts of a loyal Press, valuable as such efforts undoubtedly are in promoting and preserving it. Nor is it kept fresh and unshaken only through that inbred love of display and pageantry, characteristic of the English, who, accustomed through centuries to a good show upon meet occasions, would hate to be deprived of their pleasure in coronets and ermine, gilded coaches and martial music. Nor can it be easily and summarily explained by the splendid character of the present Royal House, who as individuals merit loyalty and affection. As her history has shown, England can behead or depose a king as wisely as she can love and honour him. Perhaps, indeed, in the very truth of this statement lies a goodly share of the reason behind that love and honour.

For even a partial understanding of that which rests at the base of these evidences of regard, esteem, and homage, it is necessary to grasp, at least in part, certain fundamental ideas and ideals of the English as a people. That aristocratic ideal under which they have been reared for centuries has at its root a reverence for tradition and a respect for superiority wherever it is found. Respect for birth, rank, and decently acquired wealth is stronger in England than elsewhere in the world; and a relatively homogeneous population living in geographical isolation has been able to preserve this attitude where other countries have failed. Unlike the upper classes of France and of Russia the ruling classes of England from the Conqueror downwards, her great families, have not brought ruin and confusion upon her people. In the exercise of their power they have been at the same time servants of the public and of the common welfare, loyal in most cases to the principle of *noblesse oblige*. In small things as the landlords of great estates they have generally dealt in fairness and friendliness with their tenants; in large matters as statesmen and diplomats they have won the confidence of those whom they have served. Since they already possess the advantages of birth, rank and wealth, it is not likely, reasons the Englishman, that they are out for personal gain; instead he sees in them his servants as well as his rulers. To him, if his basically unreflective mind should ponder the situation, the old families of his country bear much the same prestige as old, time-honoured, inviolable business firms, which have put out honest and reliable products for centuries. Hence it is but natural that the people as a whole have greater faith in the leaders of these families than in men of the lower classes. The word *gentleman* in England connotes fair dealing as well as rank and position; it is a deep-rooted idea as well as a term; and the Englishman with an instinct born of experience willingly places his trust in it.

England as a nation has never been given either to the promotion or to the admiration of mediocrity. Not for her the fallacious notion that all men are equal, even although she cherishes deeply and tenaciously the knowledge that within her boundaries all men are, and must be, free. Her ancient universities have always held as their ideal the training of superior minds for recognition and for service rather than the pathetic raising of the general intelligence. But that superior minds may well be found among the masses of her people she has been quick to recognize; and the average Englishman is secure in the knowledge that no position is closed to excellence and distinction from whatever class it may spring. Year by year the nation has seen honours given where honours are due, in scholarship and industry as well as in statesmanship, regardless of the accidents of birth or of fortune. This recognition has transmuted the envy of the great to possible emulation of them, and has tended to keep within sane bounds one of the most contented peoples on the face of the earth.

Together with a reverence for tradition and a confidence in superiority is a widespread regard, even veneration, for what is long-established and thus, at least to most minds, permanent, stable, durable. A monarchy, which from the beginning has for the most part given to its people consideration and respect, merits respect in its turn. Customs and ceremonies, display and pageantry, owe most of their appeal to the fact that they date back for centuries and have come to be taken for granted as the birthright of the English populace. Great country houses and lands, which have been for centuries in the possession of the same family, owe much of their charm to the English mind in the very fact of their age and permanence. Generations of simpler people have walked their forests on Sunday afternoon, noted with pride the arms upon their high gates, looked upon their cattle, deer, and sheep grazing upon their green lawns and in their open parks. And since the desire to own a home in the country has been from time immemorial the desire of English hearts everywhere, there is more understanding than envy in the minds of those who gaze at Knole and Raby, Longleat and Chatsworth.

This reverence for what is long-established and, therefore, durable, this respect for superiority, this taking things for granted without too much reflection upon them, this pride in age and respectability, this confidence in experience, this suspicion of innovation and experiment, have through long centuries given rise to certain ideas, not logically arrived at, but perhaps for that very reason more intact and inviolable. The English are not an analytical people. Their devotion to what has been and is their birthright, a devotion which seems enigmatical to other peoples in view of the English love of and insistence upon independence, individuality, and freedom, is to them merely a fact, natural, unanalyzed, accepted and acceptable. The King is an idea before he is a person; royalty and all its magnificence an idea rather than an ideal; and this idea, one thinks, comes in its daily application closer than most ideas to the old Platonic notion of the Universal. London is assuredly no celestial city, no *Beata Urbs;* and yet the gracious, generous spirit abroad upon its streets during the two occasions, which some of us were so privileged to witness in the past months, suggests even in this alien time Socrates' definition of that higher city possible of construction within the minds of men.

III

On the January morning immediately following the death of King George V, I rode into market on a country bus. Among the dark-clad, saddened passengers were two women who sat behind me and whose conversation was distinctly audible.

"Well, 'e's gone, Susie," said one of them to her companion. "It's 'ard to realize it, but 'e's gone."

"Death's comin' to us all," observed Susie, her black cotton gloves resignedly folded on the handle of her market basket, "to us common folks as well as to our King. I said to my 'usband this mornin', this brings it 'ome to us like. Well, there 'tis. An' when it comes, may the good Lord give us 'is own guts to meet it!"

I pondered for some moments upon Susie's rejoinder since her closing possessive was not entirely clear in its reference. But it was evident that to her and her companion the possessor of the requisite "guts" might easily have been their King as well as the Lord God Almighty!

X

An English Sunday

I

ENGLISH Sundays are marked *in aeternum* for me by the most divergent of emotions, the most profound depression in the town, the most profound pleasure in the country. London, the friendliest of cities on six days of the week, becomes on the seventh the most inhospitable, "the world forgetting, by the world forgot." Londoners who cannot get to the country for Sunday spread wide the impression that they are putting up badly with a bad job. To ask a direction from a rare wanderer through the City or on the Embankment on Sunday morning is to receive in tone and accent a commiseration which goes far toward deepening one's sense of the *Weltschmerz;* and to endure a rainy Sabbath in any of the environs of Bloomsbury (an experience too well known to numberless American students!) is to plunge oneself into a state of melancholy in which even the Hebrew prophets sound merry voices!

London is supremely careless of the comforts or the pleasures of her visitors on Sunday. If they are stupid enough to remain in town, they can take what the town offers, and it is little enough. Churches after the morning service is over are tightly locked until Evensong; and even if one goes to church at any hour from a sense of duty, of enjoyment, or of curiosity, one is somehow uncomfortably certain that the praise of the Lord is more lustily sung or spoken elsewhere than in London.

Eating on Sunday except in hotels or boarding houses entails a weary search. In Paris on a Sunday one can eat and drink in the sunlight of a pavement café. Not so in London! Pavement cafés will never come to London for the simple reason that the English do not like to eat in the open, on a city street, with a crowd of strangers, in full view of the world. When they eat in public, they like the windows to be curtained in a seemly manner so that they may not be watched by persons passing before them. Small London cafés and restaurants are for the most part closed on Sunday. When they are open, they present the disheartening spectacle, among their patrons, of others as homesick and lonely as oneself, and, among their waiters, of sombre men who give you the silent information with your tea that only grasping employers are keeping them from lying on the grass in Hyde, Green or Regent's Park where they of right ought to be.

Museums and galleries are open on Sunday, it is true, but there are few pastimes less agreeable in London as elsewhere than Sunday visits to such places. Among the crowds who throng them on that day there is, on the one hand, too much consciousness of self-improvement and, on the other, too little appreciation or intelligence.

One can ride on a bus more easily on Sundays than on other days for the reason that relatively few ride on them; but it is not a pleasant occupation, since everyone but oneself seems to be going somewhere definite and certain, and utilizing the bus only for that purpose.

Cinemas are open, and even though one may not care for them, they often prove at the close of a day of wandering the one barren island in a sea of internal storm.

Of all districts in London on a Sunday perhaps the City is the most desolate. Here the busy hum of men has lapsed into a silence sometimes more noisy. The absence of the mighty, unmeasured, never-ending stream of traffic, which on week-days marks these narrow streets, is in itself dejecting by the very force of contrast. The newspaper offices of Fleet Street are barred and still; Queen Victoria and Cannon Street offer now no objection to one's crossing at any angle or to walking straight down their middle if one desires; Bread, Milk, and Wood streets are completely deserted; and within the closely gated Inns of Court drowsy nurses sit by perambulators in which are sleeping infants too young to know what day they are enduring.

A close second for Sunday desolation are those dull and sundry streets which, lying about the British Museum, house the foreigners who labour therein to satisfy their various academic enthusiasms or necessities. At early evening these streets, Gordon Square, Tavistock and Torrington, Bedford Place and Woburn, Great Russell Street, Hart, Montague, and Gower, are punctuated by Americans traversing the distance from their rooms in boarding-houses and a hundred small hotels to the nearest red pillar-boxes to post their Sunday letters home. I know well the tenour of this evening walk and have often pondered on the heavy freight which the unsuspecting mail-trucks will carry to the General Post Office, there to be sent to the earliest ship. I know too, the rooms in which these letters were written, the sagging, chintz-covered bed, the bureau with the drawer that sticks, the view from the one window, the bowl and pitcher and hot water can, the face towel marked in red cotton, the shilling gas grate, the work-table with one leg too short, the smell of Sunday cabbage from the basement area. I know the common drawing-room, its gilt-legged tables, tuneless piano, cretonne-covered chairs, the cups and saucers in the cabinet, the sporting prints and the faces of Milton, Tennyson and Disraeli on the flowered walls, the thin slices of bread and butter and plum cake, the unattached English women who have seen better days, and the peevish American child who, unappreciative of her father's scholarship and her mother's loyalty, wishes she were at home!

Much of the dreariness of a Sunday in London lies without doubt in the attitude of the English themselves toward a city and toward city streets in general. To them the sole purpose of a city is to house those who must live and work in it, the sole function of a city street to contain the traffic, not to afford a place for a walk. They walk in the country or in parks when they cannot reach the country. For them, unlike the people of Rome or Paris or Munich, a street is no place of amusement or of entertainment. Nor is it even a place of possible beauty. It is rather a necessity, which hastens them to their work in the morning and allows them to get away quickly from it at night. The idea of spending leisure in the streets is unthinkable to them; and perhaps the melancholy which the foreign wanderer on a Sunday feels soaking into his very bones is that felt and gladly left behind by the Londoner when he escapes into the privacy of his own home or into the welcome freedom of the country.

An English Sunday should be spent whenever possible far from the town. The English railways recognize this national necessity and to supply the demand arising from it run any number of additional trains on Saturday out of London. Extra buses, too, go in all directions; and, since distances are so short even between the farthest points, the banker and the baker alike can reach the Surrey downs in an hour and the Yorkshire dales in little more than three. There is no country in the world which for its size offers such a variety of choice to the week-ender. He can wander through the bracken of the Cornish cliffs with the Atlantic pounding before him, follow the swift Devonshire streams through woodlands of ferns, foxgloves, and holly, traverse the innumerable public footpaths through the comfortable, flat fields of Essex, climb the small Cotswolds or the high fells of the lakes, watch the sunset from the Sussex marshes, lie in the heather of Dartmoor or Exmoor or the North, drink his tea under the oaks of half a dozen forests, sail on the Norfolk Broads, warm his heart under the red roofs and in the sunny hop-fields of Kent, and know in Somerset and Wiltshire every sort of land, shaven downs, rolling fields, heaths and moors, hills, copses, and gorges. Here he can view the works of the Almighty and like Him call them good, whatever the weather. And by a strange paradox, bad as English weather is, it somehow affords on the whole more hours out of doors than that of any other country. Cloudy skies do not necessarily mean rain, and although more rain falls seemingly upon this island than elsewhere in the world, there are few days without relatively rainless hours. Nor is there ever a fortnight throughout the year, even in midwinter, when the land is not green and when there is not some growth in the fields and hedges.

One wakens everywhere in rural England on Sunday to the sound of bells, which, whether or not one goes churchward early, are pleasing to the ear. At eleven o'clock after a slow breakfast and an hour in the garden one prepares for matins together with a fair representation of whatever village is the place of sojourn. Country churches on Sunday retain more of themselves and of their long past than on week-days; and an attendance upon them is always rewarding. There is at the start the walk through the churchyard, the bustle in the vestry of the village boys donning cassocks and surplices, the settling of the villagers in their seats after a moment on their knees, the opening of prayer-books and hymnals, the always exciting entrance of the gentry, sometimes even the procession of the people from a "great house" to the Family pew in the chancel or at the front.

One seldom finds untoward zeal in English country churches. There are instead a certain homeliness, an all-pervading sense that it is the proper thing to come to church, and a general atmosphere of decency and seemliness. I cannot say that I have heard many stirring or memorable sermons in them; but I have gained a great liking for English country vicars in general. The churches themselves need no eloquence from their pulpits, for there is quite sufficient in their Norman towers and fonts, their fourteenth century porches, their Tudor choir screens, their lepers' squints and old brasses, the beautiful tracery of their windows. If on Pentecost, when all country churches are decked in red and white flowers, I am more impressed by the sunlight through ancient glass than by the linguistic feats of the Parthians and Medes, Elamites and the dwellers in Mesopotamia, I am at least impressed; and if on Trinity Sunday the vicar's explanation of that mystery fails to clear up my own difficulties concerning it, I can read the monuments on the wall beside me.

Here lyeth interred
in the hope of a glorious resurrection the earthly body of
Susannah
relict of
Matthew Trowbridge, Gent.
A lady whose outward form bore pleasurable evidence of inward virtue, who possessed in abundant degree the saintly qualities of wife and mother, who, although she gave constant and unerring heed to her husband through ten years of his patient affliction, and uncomplainingly returned to God ten of her twelve children, was yet an example in homely excellence and in steadfast piety to her neighbours, keeping well the Commandments of her God, trusting in the solemn mercies of her Saviour, confident of the unfathomable grace of the Holy Ghost.
Behold a virtuous woman.

It is pleasing to me to assume that Susannah sustained no difficulties concerning the Trinity, to surmise that even though she had, she was amply justified by her good works!

Beneath these nearby Stones
Are deposited the Remains
of Ellen
Wife and Lady to Sir Henry de la Bere.
With the nobler Virtues that elevate our nature
She possessed the softer Talents that adorn it.
Pious, humble, benevolent, candid, and Sincere
She fulfilled the duties of Humanity.
And her Heart was warm with all its best Affections.
Her Sense was strong, her Judgment accurate,
Her Wit engaging and her Taste refined,
While the Elegance of her Form
The Graces of her Manner
And the natural Propriety
That ever accompanied her Words and Actions
Made her Virtues doubly attractive,
And taught her equally to command
Respect and Love.
Such She lived and such She died
Calm and resign'd to the Dispensations of Heaven,
Leaving her disconsolate Friends
To deplore her Loss
And cherish the dear Remembrance
Of that Worth
They honour'd Living
And lament in Death.

To the Memory of the best of Wives, the best of Friends
He for whom She joined those tender Names
Dedicates this marble.

She was married on Nov. 10th, 1765, at the age of sixteen,
And died in Childbed Aug. 15th, 1766.

Ellen's brief years and the ironic burden of her untimely fate, coupled with eloquence such as this, supply meet meditation for many quiet minutes in a country church!

The King, the Queen, the Duke and the Duchess of York and all other members of the Royal Family entrusted to God, the Psalms sung with country warmth, the prayers said, the sermon preached, and the smallest choir boy aroused from his slumbers, friends and neighbours are greeted in the churchyard, healths are enquired, and the congregation slowly disperses for roast beef and port, for chicken and champagne, or for ham and boiled potatoes, steak and kidney pie, sausages and black puddings.

On fair Sunday afternoons all rural England is in the fields and lanes or on the cricket grounds, young and old, dogs and children, lovers and sweethearts, perambulators and doll buggies. The rivers at Oxford and Cambridge in the spring are thick with undergraduates in punts and canoes; fishermen stand on the rocks above the Wye and the Severn; the great trees along the Dee shelter families with tea-baskets; the bridges over the Ouse, the Stour, the Wensum, the Frome, the Avon, the Parret, the Brue, are thronged with small boys avid for dace and shiners. At Epping and in the New Forest Lon-

doners come into their own after a week of tolera-
tion; on the Yorkshire moors mill-hands forget their
hours at the looms. Great houses everywhere open
their lawns and woods to the populace at large, who
throng by thousands to catch a glimpse of life far
different from their own.

At six o'clock in the country anywhere one can
hardly find himself out of the sound of a peal of bells
ringing for Evensong. Not the slow, sonorous, reverberating tones of French bells for England, but peal
upon peal ringing out across the meadows and over
the slow rivers. At this hour traffic on the roads
assumes major proportions; not the motor traffic, for
most cars are parked in woods and fields, but the
foot traffic of villagers walking homeward or to
church. Evensong in the country has a social as well
as a religious aspect, and village churches are far
more crowded for that service than in the morning.

The English unlike the Americans are not a people who drive through the country for the sake of
driving. They like destinations, secure and certain,
with a cup of tea and an hour's walk once they are
reached in the afternoon, or with a long day before
them if they can arrive at their goal in the morning.
The Englishman is not a long distance driver or, by
nature, a long distance traveller of any sort; and the

casual **American** who thinks nothing of hundreds of miles by train or motor is amazing to him. He buys a car to get him to the country, and when he is once there, the car in itself has little charm for him.

In June it is light until nearly eleven. I have read on the Cornish coast until then, and on the first day of summer have seen a last pink cloud over Gloucester cathedral as the clocks were striking that hour. At ten-thirty on fair days the horizon glows with the last of the sunset, and the night itself is but four hours in duration. With a Sunday of sixteen hours at least before him, it is only the most stupid and un-English of men who will stay in town if there is any means of leaving it. For the country to the English does not beckon them so much as it belongs to them, does not offer them a welcome change from the town so much as it expects them to claim their own. They are somehow by nature a part of it, and their enforced habitation away from it is but a sufferance.

The existence of the eighteenth century "man about town" was an artificial existence in an artificial period. Fielding subsisted in London but lived in Somerset, within his books and out; and Sir Roger de Coverley was and in modern dress still *is* the ideal of nine-tenths of the English nation.

XI

English Railway Travel

I

ALTHOUGH the majority of visitors to England now quite wisely bring or hire motor-cars for seeing the country, there is not a little to be said for the older method of the third-class railway carriage. Here one surely comes more closely into connection with the people at large; here at small cost one can see a vast deal of the country itself.

Moreover, automobile travel robs one of that desultory waiting at the station, characteristic of English travellers, who like to allow plenty of time. I know of no greater amusement or pleasure than to linger about Paddington or Waterloo on the eve of a Bank Holiday. The dinginess of a London railway terminus is in itself a welcome change from the smart cleanliness, perfection, and even beauty of the Grand Central or the Pennsylvania Station, either of which would strike awe, amazement, and incredulity in the mind of the ordinary English traveller.

There is surely nothing smart about Paddington, nothing perfect about Waterloo, nothing beautiful about Liverpool Street, and nothing overly clean about any of them. Nevertheless, there is about all of them, in contrast to most American stations, a pleasing homogeneity and stability; and they seem to suffice the English, who after all are mostly bent upon getting into the country.

That the English still take their holidays in general *en famille,* their two weeks' summer holiday or their shorter jaunts at Easter, Whitsun, or during the early August recess, is clearly apparent at the stations. Here they are, the satisfied father in flannels, the more agitated mother, who has perforce hastily dressed, the daughter in her broad-brimmed straw or felt and her long black cotton stockings, the son in school coat and cap, and the small boy in gray shorts with a sailing-boat under his arm. The dog is often along, for dogs are more closely inbred in English families than in American, frequent appendages in England rather than infrequent accessories at home. Their luggage is about, upon, and beside them, sundry suit-cases of fibre or pasteboard or worn leather, baskets with lunch and bathing-costumes, umbrellas, tennis racquets, boxes and bundles of sorts. English luggage in general rarely delights the fastidious eye and never less so than when it is carrying the family clothing to the seaside.

Upturned suit-cases form convenient seats in the over-crowded stations. Last Christmas at Paddington in a pea-soup fog, when trains were from one to three hours late both in arrival and departure, hundreds of people sat about upon their luggage, talking good-humouredly one group with another and perching innumerable cups of tea wherever space and convenience offered. No one seemed in the least upset or even annoyed by the summary change in their plans which the sudden fog had made; porters with holly in their button-holes moved about as though time were not; and a race-horse, waiting for his loose box on a late train, was led up and down the station platform to the great interest of all those similarly delayed. Green clouds of fog occasionally swept down from the roofing, the atmosphere became each moment more smoky and intolerable on throat and eyes, the obscurity perceptibly thickened so that at times only one's nearest neighbours were discernible, the air was wet and cold; yet, as I surveyed this miserable situation, I could ascertain no one but myself visibly annoyed in the least.

Third-class carriages on the eve of Bank Holidays are crowded to the doors and windows, their corridors similarly so. Wet woollen is not a pleasant smell, and woollen in England throughout most of the year is wet on a conservative average of four days out of seven. Nevertheless, good nature abounds on English railway trains; and one is sure to miss a great deal in this country unless he at times at least affords himself their pleasurable features.

One of these is the responsibility which the English guards, or conductors, take of all those journeying under their care. Tickets are punched in England more often than in any other country I know, carefully scrutinized, and returned with the reassurance that you are actually on your right train. Moreover, before the train starts, a courteous official goes its length and breadth and inquires through the window of the corridor whether or not you are bound for the place you think you are. This relieves you from any anxiety and enables you to cherish your absent-mindedness in perfect peace.

At town and country stations you are again set right in your mind by local guards, who usually wear flowers in their button-holes and constantly emanate contentment and the sense of leisure. These men are always concerned over whether or not you are supplied with tea, especially if the train has no restaurant car. They will procure you a tea-basket for two shillings or less, or summon a white-coated boy with a tea-wagon, who will hand you through the window a steaming cup, together with a roll of excellent biscuits, for sixpence. You may drink your tea at leisure and then push your cup and saucer beneath your portion of the long seat, trusting to the Great Western or the London and Northeastern to recover their property whenever and wherever they feel like doing so.

There is no checking system for large pieces of luggage in England. This lack sometimes lends anxiety to the foreigner until he penetrates farther into the nature of English porters and into the honesty of the country in general. Your trunk or larger suit-case is placed in a luggage van, the location of which the porter reveals to you as he approaches you with his empty truck to say good-bye. He says it is quite safe at the farther end of the second van behind your carriage next a perambulator and a crate of eggs, and that you have only to apprise the porter of this information at your stopping-off place. This information you give to the porter at your stopping-off place, sometimes accompanying him into the van to discover it precisely as you were told next the perambulator and the eggs.

I have certainly spent some enviable hours in English third-class carriages. Aside from the delight of seeing the green country slip past with its fine trees, grazing cattle, gray-towered churches and snug villages, aside from the pleasure of being admonished at most of the station platforms that if I am weakly, I must take Bovril daily, I have greatly enjoyed my fellow passengers. For one thing, their reading always interests me. The average English traveller, especially among the women, is not given to magazines so much as to certain books. Although one frequently sees *The Argosy, True Romances,* and *The Happy Magazine,* one forever sees those sixpenny and nine-penny volumes common to English news-stands and immensely popular in third-class carriages. Since at most there are but eight persons in a carriage, one is often in close proximity to one's neighbours; and I have done much entertaining reading by quick glances either to my right or left. I remember my sense of frustration one morning last winter when I had caught over my neighbour's shoulder these words: "Mrs. Van der Ruyter's life was tragically changed that brilliant June morning when Captain Gillespie brought her the inlaid casket from Hindostan." My companion took Mrs. Van der Ruyter and the captain with her when she left the train at Bishops Stortford, and I am still in the dark! Zane

Grey, Edgar Wallace, and Ethel M. Dell are popular associates in third-class carriages. So is Tarzan in his various portrayals. Ethel never fails to stir my sense of appreciation and acknowledgment; for once, when I was ill in England for a month, I read a complete set of her books belonging to my nurse. I know her better and more entirely than I know any other author, since she was then my only literary resource; and I am always conscious of what I owe to her. Her stories and those of Mr. Grey and Mr. Wallace are not, however, at least according to my researches in third-class carriages, the most beloved. This distinction I would unhesitatingly assign to Ruby M. Ayres since I see her name most frequently. She is the author of numerou. books with stirring titles such as *A Gamble with Love, The Second Honeymoon, Brown Sugar,* and *The Remembered Kiss.* A sale of several hundred thousand copies of any one of her successes is, I am told, nothing to Miss Ayres. Second to her in extreme popularity are May Christie with *The Rebel Bride* and *The Gilded Rose* and a certain Miss June Dawn with *Jealousy!* There is also a certain series of twopenny romances called *True Love Series,* four numbers of which are issued every month. Since these are even less expensive than those of Miss Ayres, Miss Christie and Miss Dawn, one often sees their lurid covers and their intriguing titles, *Because She Was Proud, The Bride of an Hour,* and *Betrayed by Her Friend.* These volumes do not seem to stir in men the same answering appeal. They read the papers, the *Times,* the *Telegraph,* the *Mail,* the *Standard,* the *Mirror,* and thus, to a certain degree, mark themselves and their stations in English society.

It would not be fair, of course, or accurate to suggest that the reading in railway carriages is relegated to the sixpenny, ninepenny or twopenny thriller, which, one must always remember, differs only in quality, not in kind, from that which we term literature. In the hands of all sorts of people one naturally sees all sorts of books; but it is true, I think, that such inexpensive reading matter, largely because of its wider publication in England than elsewhere, is more generally read at least on trains by those who, like all of us, are after emotional satisfaction in their reading, but who do not miss the lack of art in its handling.

Then, too, I have made on English trains the acquaintance of many persons whom I shall never see again but who have given me pleasure for a chance hour and agreeable memories thereafter. Once on a journey from Cambridge to Lincoln I shared my otherwise empty carriage with a chicken girl. Fascinated by a catalogue she was perusing, which showed all manner of fowls and advertised foods certain to produce manifold and maximum eggs, I offered her an American cigarette in the hope of inducing conversation. She was delighted with the cigarette, the like of which together with a *bona fide* American she had never seen before, and forthwith gave me amazing information about her lifework. She said it was utter nonsense that one manner of fowl could not be made to breed with another. Her mother, she swore, possessed positive magic with every sort of farmyard poultry, and had brought forth from the successful and happy combination of a turkey and a duck such a creature as even Whipsnade or Regent's Park might envy. When she left the train at a way-station in the vicinity of Lincoln, she invited me with such cordiality to come and see this marvel that for several perilous moments I wavered between the turkey-duck and the cathedral.

In travelling to Somerset one afternoon I met an English couple with a surprising array of little girls ranging from five years to six months. I have always remembered their names, Gillian, Greta, Audrey, Susan, and Marilyn, and have often since wondered about Susan, a quiet, sober child, twin to Greta, and seemingly unequally yoked. I have other and far more serious reason to recall this family at anxious intervals, for, attempting in some way to return their friendliness, I distributed five American pennies among them. To our combined horror the head of Abraham Lincoln disappeared almost instantly down the throat of Marilyn, the baby. She seemed, however, to suffer no disastrous effects from this debasement of the American coinage; and I can only hope she has survived to justify the quickly regained serenity of her English parents.

Often on English trains the very ill-assortment of persons is in itself intriguing. Once in the station at Reading an impeccable English clergyman entered my carriage and gave himself up immediately to the reading of a large volume entitled *Hours with the Mystics*. From the gold cross suspended on a chain, which went from one of his waistcoat-pockets to the other, I judged him to be of High Church persuasion and felt for the moment uneasy over *The Saturday Evening Post* which I had purchased at exorbitant cost from the news-stand in London. Just before the train started, a somewhat harassed elderly woman entered with a bunch of garden flowers, which had evidently been presented to her by the friend and contemporary who was seeing her off.

"Don't worry about Handrew, Tillie," said the friend through the carriage window. "Just tell 'im to 'ang on to the Lord with might an' main. 'E never fails us! 'E'll be a crutch an' a life-line to Handrew, 'e will. 'Is grace is mighty to save. Tell Handrew that."

The clergyman was evidently perturbed and a bit embarrassed by this intrusion of realism into his mystical meditations. He apparently cared as little for the mixed metaphors of Tillie's friend as for her somewhat rude application of emotions dealt with in a more seemly and cautious manner by the mystics! At all events the expression on his face is not to be forgotten.

The most memorable of my experiences in third-class carriages, however, was vouchsafed me on a corridor-less, non-stop train from Southampton to Waterloo. Prior to this journey, I had always taken an especial delight in corridor-less trains particularly on non-stop journeys; for if travel is light and you are lucky, you are often assured of a compartment entirely to yourself. Here you may sleep, sew, remake your appearance, wander from one end of the carriage to the other, and know for a season complete and inviolable privacy. This was, unfortunately, not destined to be my portion on the morning a year ago when I bought my ticket for Waterloo; for, just as the train was beginning to move, an anxious and somewhat dishevelled man between youth and middle age jumped aboard my carriage and seated himself breathlessly in the corner opposite my own. He bore a somewhat battered small leather case, which he almost immediately opened to draw therefrom a sheaf of heavily pencilled manuscript. Apparently resenting my presence, he hurriedly glanced with distressed eyes about the compartment; then, understanding that there was no exit possible for me except upon the railway tracks, he began reading his manuscript to himself in muttered undertones. I gathered that, whatever the nature of his composition, it weighed heavily upon his mind, and moved to the other end of the compartment, urged there not only by his evident agitation but also by the wildness of his appearance in general.

After a few minutes of husky oratory, he asked my permission to read aloud, saying that he was rehearsing a speech for an open air meeting somewhere in London. He thanked me for my uneasy acquiescence, saying as he did so that he hoped I would be in hearty agreement with his sentiments and opinions and that he would be glad of any suggestion from me. Although I have forgotten most of the oration, which I listened to with mounting terror, one sentence remains ineradicably in my mind, for it caused confusion between us.

"Spreading throughout the world the only hope for crushed humanity, shining like a beacon light over a mad sea of oppression, the Conservative Party seeks to annihilate the ideals of Holy Russia."

This sentence was apparently revered by him as his high moment, for he read it again with increasing excitement before he turned upon me.

"What do you think of that?" he shouted, rising in his frenzy and approaching my end of the compartment. "I say, won't that get them? What do you think of that?"

Some answer being obviously required of me, I made in my own extreme excitement a fatal reply.

"It sounds wonderful," I said, "but are you quite sure the participles are where they should be?"

"Participles! Participles!" yelled he. "What do you mean—participles?"

"I mean," I ventured as calmly as I could, "are you sure the meaning is clear? Wouldn't one perhaps think that the Conservative Party instead of Holy Russia did the spreading of hope, was the beacon, so to speak, over the mad sea of oppression?"

"Madam!" he screamed, now hanging from the luggage rack and glowering down at me. "Don't you believe in holy justice?"

"I certainly do," I stammered, wondering if to jump from a moving train were necessarily fatal. "Justice at all costs."

"If justice was established on this earth," he cried, now swinging from the rack, "charity would die a natural death!"

This sentiment apparently exhausted him, for he mercifully withdrew to his corner and continued his reading in an undertone, not deigning even so much as another glance in my direction.

Since this experience I have considered the English railways wise in their growing abolition of corridor-less trains. Nevertheless, it has heightened rather than lessened my fondness and regard for railway travel in general, and through it I have learned that pedantry has no legitimate place in a third-class carriage—or elsewhere!

XII

The Spring in England

I

THIS year I followed upon the heels of the spring in France from late March until mid-April. The lilacs and cherries, quinces, magnolias and Judas trees of Provence had dropped their blossoms when on Easter morning in the green fields and gardens of Isère they were in full flower. Two days later in the small dark valleys of the Jura the close purple buds of the lilacs were only just flushing with violet, the fruit trees by the small swift streams only just showing their white petals. The Isère poplars shimmered in full leaf in the spring sunlight, which in Flanders had brought but the first hint of green to their upright branches. Late March starred the high fields of La Grande Chartreuse with primroses; mid-April gave them to the Flemish dikes at the same hours when cowslips had taken their places on Carthusian slopes. And during the bleak days following Easter in Reims one must perforce be content with the less secure immortality of the innumerable leaves carved in stone on the walls and capitals of her cathedral.

One could not thus follow the spring in England. Primroses, it is true, come a bit earlier on the high, green banks of Devonshire and at the foot of Somerset hedges than they do in the Midlands and the north, thanks to the milder Channel winds and brighter sunlight of the south. They are sold on dark March days in London for twopence a bunch and taken home by thousands of city workers to brighten dingy, fog-swept rooms. Yet this little world of England is in itself too small to afford the variations of France, her valleys too shallow, her mountains and hills too low, her climate in general too similar from Northumberland to Kent; and although the snowdrops in the gardens of the south may be some days earlier than those farther north, the long, slow coming of the English spring is relatively the same within the four hundred miles of quiet country between the Sussex marshes and the Tweed.

The arrival of spring in most of America is sudden, bursting upon us one April day when we are sick to death of sodden snow, cold March winds, reluctant trees. We wake one morning to a new warmth in the air, to the sound of dripping eaves, and to a sun whose heat by noon has opened our coats and made us call excitedly to friends on the streets that spring is really here. Following a night of warm rain, dandelions glow in the new grass; orchards bloom and fade in one short week of sudden warmth; song sparrows give place to thrushes before we are aware.

This is not England's way. Her tardy spring does not appear in any such vivacious manner, has none of the swift, breath-taking qualities of that at home, although it is prodigal beyond words when it is once upon her. It begins its leisurely unfolding in late January, braving some of the worst weather this island can produce; it saves its completeness for the entire month of May when the whole land slowly spreads itself in bloom. One can, therefore, watch minutely its beginnings, its retardings, its progress step by step, for literally four months of the new year. For this reason it is in England the most rewarding of seasons, dilatory and unhurried, spacing its surprises comfortably and well.

By the last week of January the snowdrops and the aconites have reared their heads in garden plots everywhere. Sometimes stiff with frost in the morning, sometimes buried in a night's wet snowfall, by noon they are limber and jaunty enough and apparently quite unharmed. In January on the high

Northumberland fields above the sea the gulls follow the farmer's plough in great clouds of white as he turns a darker earth than the warm reds that mark the soil of the Midlands and the south. By February in and above the fields of winter grain or of stubble the skylarks are singing. On a day of warmth and sunlight they fill the air with music, now almost a high monotony like that which at home is made by the high shrilling of crickets in autumn, now, when they leave the ground to shoot upward and out of sight, a sudden crescendo of unimaginable variation falling in trills and quavers from sky to earth. By February, too, the blackbirds and thrushes have abandoned their mid-winter silence and the minor notes of their November songs for full-throated calls and carollings from the blackthorn hedges, just beginning to show their first faint traces of white. The backs of the Cambridge colleges in February are royal with the gold and purple of thousands upon thousands of crocuses. They carpet the green lawns of Trinity and King's, follow the quiet backwashes of the river, catch and hold and scatter the sunlight of rare warm mornings.

In March the ewes are put out into the meadows to await their lambs. This certain sign of awakening life is more encouraging to those who watch than is the new but reluctant growth of the hedgerows, which seem to change little from day to day. Enclosures are built for them, and the rectangular, box-like lambing-hut of the shepherd, lumbering along the country roads, takes up its station in the center of the fields. The shepherds, I am told, receive the sum of ninepence for each lamb brought to a sufficiently secure maturity; and like Gabriel Oak they work early and late at their lonely midwifery. March and April midnights in the country are filled with the bleatings of ewes and new lambs; and if one lives fortunately near a lambing meadow as I have for two years past, there is small want of entertainment for six weeks on end. Lambs in every stage of life lie or stagger, frisk or leap, suck or sleep from early dawn until late twilight, the stout long-legged lambs of Northamptonshire and Huntingdon, the smaller ones of Somerset and Wilts. There is more than the picturesque or the amusing in this pastoral scene which is enacted every spring; for these long meadows throughout England have to no small extent contributed to her history for well-nigh a thousand years.

Slowly the spring comes on its way, retreating before days of cold rain and weeks of blustering wind. But the vanguards tenaciously remain as an earnest

—snowdrops, aconites, and crocuses, early blossoming plums, the frail lavender flowers of the rosemary, the first green of the hedges. By April there is a larger hope. Now the king-cups open in the marshes; the cowslips, "paigles" as the country people call them, fill the meadows and the hands of country children; celandines blossom by the streams and ditches; and "lords and ladies" begin to sit under their canopies of green. Daffodils by thousands take the place of crocuses along the Cambridge backs beneath the sweeping willows; ladies' smocks silver the fields everywhere, now as by the Avon three centuries ago. The flat bulb lands of Lincolnshire, glowing with yellow, purple, and scarlet beneath the pale sky, vie with Holland in their wealth and brightness.

In the gardens of old cottages and of new council houses men and women dig in the evenings which, now that the time has changed, afford light until nine o'clock. These small gardens are one of the most wholesome and beautiful features of English village life. There is literally no house, however mean, without its wall-flowers, tulips, forget-me-nots, and pansies. Conversation is exchanged over gates and hedges, comparisons made; swappings take place between this garden and that, superfluous roots and seedlings from one going to people the bare spaces of another. Men engaged all day in various trades and jobs like to turn in the evening to a bit of gardening; and the effect all summer throughout rural England not only amply repays them for their labour but helps to make imperishable that sentiment which has for so long surrounded the English village.

At five o'clock one mid-April morning one is suddenly awakened by the cuckoo, calling from far across the fields, invisible in his covert. And now, one says, spring *has* come. There is no longer any question. The cuckoo is everywhere accepted as the proof. As the days advance, he is the most ubiquitous of birds. From one place or another, always baffling the seeker, he calls from dawn till dark. Warm mid-days are his delight and drowsy afternoons. Taught by Wordsworth and other English friends of his charm, I had long counted him one of the major reasons for watching a spring in England. But I have seen days when, encompassed by a quite substantial and un-faery-like world of work, I have many times cried with Wordsworth, "O blessed bird!" although the emotion that fills me and the connotation within my harassed words are far different from his own!

Now spring hastens on toward her fulfilment. There is no stopping her. The dingy market-places of the county towns glow with flowers: daffodils at fourpence a bunch, poet's narcissus at sixpence, anemones like those at Epidaurus, forget-me-nots, tulips, hyacinths, and pansies to be bought for a song; stout seedlings of every description to bring summer gardens more quickly into bloom; bunches of purple-pointed asparagus for romantic natures, sick of cauliflower, cabbage and brussels sprouts; English strawberries grown under glass for those who can afford them; spruce lettuces to take the place of the inert and sluggish January variety; onions and radishes, and jaunty bundles of fresh watercress. There is spring in the cries of the vendors: " 'Ere you are, ladies! Daffodils to cheer your 'eart. Who'll take 'ome a bunch at tuppence, for mother or for sweet'eart, or the old?" A young boy selling cowslips is not behind his elders in the rhythm of his cries: "Cowslips, fresh cowslips, the sign o' spring! Picked early in the meadows by me own 'and!"

Now the orchards and hillsides, woodlands and spinneys and copses come into their own. Apples in Kent and Dorset are white and crimson with bloom, heavy with the sound of bees; the blackthorn and wild plum edge the fields everywhere with drifts of white; the spotless, pendant blossoms of the cherry literally hang its branches with snow, the white, clinging snow of a New England April; the gorse blows in mounds of yellow on heath and moorland, and the early heather begins to show its first faint traces of violet. Trees put out their flowers, red, green, and yellow, waiting for the first days of May to form and shape their leaves.

Spring is on the streets of city, town, and village. On London squares and corners the flower-carts shed brightness. Undergrounds and buses carry blossom-laden people homeward from their work; for the English carry flowers less self-consciously than any other people in the world. Late April brings out the blue and the white tricycles of the ice cream vendors, those good-natured blue- or white-coated men, treadling behind the succinct sign which says, "Stop Me and Buy One". The fish-and-chips peddler, rattling through the villages in the early evening, gives an extra pennyworth of sizzling chips to the small boys who leave their cricket to encircle his smoking van. There is an added lilt in the cry of the North Country boot-mender as he trundles past in his swaying cart: "Boots? Boots? Is owt wrong with your boots?" Men now drink their evening ale and beer not within the public-house but without, sitting with their pipes and mugs on the benches beneath the sign of *The Blue Boar, The Sow and Pigs, The Black Duck,* or *The Green Man.* And those misguided minds who think the English an unsentimental race have but to note how in the hours between tea and supper lovers sit beneath the hedges, or later, with arms about each other's waists, start for the cinema, there to see the supplement, the complement, or the consummation of their own seasonal heart-stirrings!

But it is May which completes the long travail of the spring. There is nothing elsewhere that I know even remotely resembling this month in England. By May the spring is at its full. The wonder is that it is held so long in its completeness, that its flood tide does not diminish. It is now that the English climate is justified, now that the soaking, driving rains of January, February, and March absolve themselves. Old Thales, had he lived in England, might have been amply bolstered up in his contention that the beginning of all things lies in water! In England such miracles are not instantaneous but long drawn out, thanks to a climate which has no early heat to wither and consume what her slow spring has taken so long to bring to birth.

Lilacs in May hang over garden walls and hedges in veritable weeks of bloom, even while quinces, forsythia, lauristinus, pink flowering currants, and Judas trees retain their April freshness. The splendour of apples and cherries, plums and pears, in this island is not a short but a long perfection. Now comes the red and the white may in close masses of starry flowers, making the whole land rejoice; now comes, too, the laburnum, golden chains, the children call it, to hang its clusters over thousands of hedges and transform a pale gray day into sunshine. Horse-chestnuts, Whitsun trees, lift their pyramids of white and rose, touched indeed by Pentecostal flames. From the crannies of old walls everywhere throughout the south, from the sea wall of St. Ives in Cornwall, above the high, narrow lanes of Devonshire, the valerian blossoms, a mass of rose and white lasting far into July. The purple spikes of veronica catch their own reflection in the shining mirror of their leaves; wallflowers are persistent tongues of fire in every garden; and along the wide avenues of great country houses like that of Longleat in Wiltshire the rhododendrons begin to show their pink, white, and purple.

Not behind the gardens in their array are the common hedgerows everywhere. For they flaunt the

Union Jack in the red of wild crane's bill, the blue
of the speedwell, and the white of stitchwort. Blue-
bells carpet the ground of Madingley Wood, and
above them on still, warm midnights the night-
ingale sings until dawn. The roadsides are tangled
with the frail white of Queen Anne's lace; the green
of the fields is lost in the white and crimson of the
low English daisy and the yellow of buttercups; and
over the ploughed lands the spring crops stretch in
orderly rows, straight and level in the east, climbing
the high, patchwork hills of Cornwall, billowing
over the undulating fields of the Midlands and of
Kent.

It is for these, one thinks, that the people of this
island endure her climate, knowing that in this sure
and certain coming of the Holy Ghost they are
saved indeed. And not alone are they in the country
vouchsafed a new and abundant life. Into the outlying residence districts of London with their rows
upon rows of indiscriminate, ugly houses, even into
the dreary lines of brick and stone that stretch in all
directions from the textile and mining centers of
England, May penetrates in some degree. Now it is
that that desire, so dear to the Englishman, to name
his home is in a measure understood. To insist upon
a name rather than a number, to call one's cottage

or one's villa, so exactly like its dull and miserable neighbour, *Hazelmere, Lilycroft, Woodville, Fernmead, Glendale, Highfields* (all of which names I have seen in the outskirts of London) seems in December and January only absurd or pathetic, only at best to emphasize that sense of individuality so stubbornly characteristic of all Englishmen everywhere. But when a warm May evening brings out the plumber from *Lilycroft* and the joiner from *Fernmead,* each to dig in his six square feet of frontal space, when the black knobs of the slow planes are at last tufted with new green, and the thin, undernourished branches of a sickly fruit tree bear a few struggling blossoms, when the sun streams through the grayness upon boys on the pavement with their tops and marbles and roller-skates, then it is that *Hazelmere* and *Lilycroft, Woodville* and *Fernmead, Glendale* and *Highfields* assume a new significance in the imagination. Their absurdity fades, even their pathos is transcended, in the understanding that, stronger even than his innate sense of his own roof-tree, is the Englishman's insistence upon the country-side as his birthright. It is this birthright which triumphs over brick and mortar, city dumps and railway tracks, which places flowers in tubs from Mayfair to Southwark, which decorates even the bare spaces between the chimney-pots on the roofs of Stepney and Shoreditch, Lambeth and Bethnal Green. The name of *Lilycroft,* one suddenly knows, must have been engendered on some clear May evening over a high tea of eggs and kippers and steaming cups of Lyons' at tuppence the packet!

XIII

On a Bus in Somerset

I

READERS of Thomas Hardy will recall the sinister thread of destiny which lends its shadow to the tapestry of so many of his novels, *Jude the Obscure, The Mayor of Casterbridge, A Pair of Blue Eyes, The Return of the Native,* and above all, to the beautifully conceived pattern which is *Tess of the D'Urbervilles.* From the fatal message in the prick of Alec D'Urberville's roses on the Blackmoor coach to those last sombre hours at Stonehenge when destiny fulfils itself, Tess knows that she cannot escape her fate, which by means of manifold signs, omens, and tokens, born of country lore and nourished in country minds, has been clear to her from the beginning. Her pathetic scrutiny of "lords and ladies" in the field, the portentous rumbling of the D'Urberville coach, the refusal of the cows to give down their milk and of the butter to "come", the trembling of the ivy outside her casement—

all of these give to her the assurance that from her birth the dice of the Gods have been loaded against her.

This same fatalism is portrayed also in that rural painting, *Under the Greenwood Tree,* lightly and more humourously woven, it is true, but yet unmistakable.

"Ay, your parson comes by fate," says Reuben Dewy, the tranter. " 'Tis heads or tails like pitch halfpenny, and no choosing; so we must take 'en as he is, my sonnies, and thank God he's no worse."

The "coming man" to Mrs. Robert Penny on Midsummer Eve was Penny, the shoemaker, much as she preferred John Wildway. Setting out the bread and cheese and beer as the witch's book ordered, she opened her door when the clock struck twelve to behold a little, small man in her lane with a shoemaker's apron on and to know that her unwelcome way lay straight before her face.

Old Enoch, the trapper in Yalbury Wood, reminds young Dick Dewy that " 'tis to be" with such force and assurance that Dick, although he is of a younger generation, speaks at once of the "doom" that settles either marriage or the single state.

And Mrs. Penny, since Midsummer Eve securely yoked to Penny in spite of herself, again accords to

Fate the credit for her resigned behaviour at the time of her wedding.

"Well, thinks I, 'tis to be, and here goes. And do you do the same: Say 'tis to be, and here goes! 'Twill carry a body through it all from wedding to church-ing, if you only let it out with spirit enough."

In the secluded valleys and villages of the West Country this same sense of destiny, classic in Hardy's treatment of it in spite of simpler surroundings, doubtless Celtic in its origin, this unanalyzed per-ception of acting in a play, the progress and con-clusion of which are already foreordained by certain immutable rules, is still apparent and lends to many of the country people a kind of acceptance in the finality of circumstances which is both pathetic and reassuring as one ponders upon it.

There is a common expression lingering on in this part of England (perhaps in other parts as well although I have run across it more often here than elsewhere) which sums up the whole matter briefly and concisely, drawing together a dozen emotions and tying them neatly into one bundle. "There 'tis," the country people say when some untoward event shatters their sense of stability or when some chain of circumstances tightens closely about its victim. "There 'tis." Sometimes more voluble tongues com·

plete the sentence: "There 'tis, and there's an end to't." But more often the two words stand by themselves in succinct and weighty finality.

I have caught this expression any number of times in overheard conversations between country people on buses, in trains, in wayside tea-gardens, in small inns, and have met with it myself as I have talked with chance acquaintances. Its insistence is, perhaps, upon the present rather than, like Mrs. Penny's, upon the future; and for that reason it holds within itself even a more significant suggestion of acceptance of the inevitable, an acceptance so close at hand that there is no possibility either of propitiating the Immortals or of escape by means of one's own designs.

II

The most perfect rendering of it and the most fitting situation for its use were vouchsafed me one August morning when I boarded a country bus in the Somerset village of Holcombe on my way to Bath. I gathered from the conversation of my fellow passengers that several were bound for a hospital in Bath, which maintained a free clinic for out-patients: and the signs of ill health and of minor past accidents about me strengthened this assumption.

At a country cross-roads a short distance farther on two women entered. One was stout and comfortable in appearance, obviously quite recovered from whatever illness she had undergone; the other was quite as obviously very ill, bearing unmistakably in her eyes and in the lines of her gaunt face the sure and steady approach of death. Each was encumbered with a profusion of garden flowers, which they placed with great care upon their laps as they took the side seat directly in front and to right angles of my own.

Their flowers immediately attracted my attention. The stout woman had arranged hers upon a wire frame in the shape of a cross. Roses and marigolds, snapdragons and the amputated heads of magenta phlox, they could not have presented a more bizarre or hideous combination of colour. But that the stout woman was secure in her pride of them and of their unique arrangement and that her companion was clearly envious were at once apparent in the care of the one and in the covetous gaze of the other. The bouquet of the thin, pale woman was beautiful in its simple distribution of blue love-in-a-mist with yellow daisies; and I felt suddenly sorry that the wire contraption of her neighbour could so plunge her into a depressing comparison. I gathered that the flowers of each were intended as a present to the same nurse in the Bath hospital, and that she who had not long to live had suddenly and cruelly been forced to undervalue her own gift.

Evidently neighbours or at least acquaintances, they began at once in the dialect of rural Somersetshire to comment upon their respective offerings.

"They be a present for Sister?" asked the pale-faced woman as though she might as well know the worst and be done with it.

The stout woman nodded in confirmation. To do her justice she was simple in her own conceit.

"Aye," she said. "They be. I thought as how she'd like a bit of a present. The cross I'd saved from me ol' father's funeral flowers, and I fixed it up like. But," she added generously, "it's all in the first look. She'll put yours in a jug in her room. Them'll last for days, them will."

Her companion was clearly unconvinced. It was easy to see that the cross represented to her extra thought and labour, a finished thing suggesting not only care but something approaching the art of a real florist's shop in town where people paid good money for such triumphs. The contrast between her own simple flowers and the set piece of her neighbour, grotesque and fantastic though it was, was a bitter recognition, ironic and hard to bear. Her eyes left the flowers to rest upon the fleeting countryside where the harvested fields lay under the pale sunshine and the autumn crocuses had begun to blossom on the roadside banks. She said no more at the moment, but there were obvious in the sudden sagging of her shoulders and of the lines in her face the acknowledgment and the accompanying resignation which she had been forced to accept.

III

The bus rattled on toward Bath. The conductor collected his big pennies in the brown leather bag slung across his shoulders, rattling them heavily for change whenever a newcomer proffered a shilling or half a crown. We jostled one another good-naturedly as we swayed and clattered on with people talking of crops and village gossip, markets and fairs, the prices of things to eat and to wear, and the happy expectations of the Duke and Duchess of Kent.

My two neighbours on the side seat, after the thin woman had accepted the situation with which she had been so cruelly confronted, fell themselves into talk about the nurse in Bath who had tended them both. I understood that in each she had not only aroused the deepest and most unqualified devotion, but that she had been the means of affording to both a wider experience than they had heretofore known in their Somerset cottages. They exchanged surmises upon this patient and that whom they had known in their hospital ward, enjoying alike as they did so extreme commiseration as well as pleasurable relief. I realized, as I listened, something of what their hospital sojourn with all its probable suffering had meant to them—the opportunity of lying in comfortable beds which they themselves had not made, between clean sheets which they had not washed and ironed, of eating food which they had not prepared; the freedom from children and inconvenient kitchens and hard work; the chance to lie all day in cleanliness and quiet with nurses to wait upon them; the memorable assurance of the brief importance which often only illness can confer upon the poor. While they had been in Bath, others had performed their tasks at home. They had been the subjects of interested conversation and village sympathy in the public-house during the evening and in the sitting-rooms of their neighbours over a cup of tea; the most recent news of them had been exchanged over garden hedges. Perhaps the vicar had even asked prayers in church for their recovery.

All this, I knew, would in the future afford pleasure to the stout woman who was soon to be well and bustling about her kitchen. Her operation, what the doctor had said to her, the solicitude of the Sister in charge and of her various nurses would form the shining center of her world until some other woman, journeying also toward Bath in search of help for her own ills, should oust her from her little day of fame.

The bus still lurched on. We left the more open countryside and saw in the distance the high green hills above Bath, set with fine trees, open now and then by the greener lawns of some great estate. I saw the eyes of the thin woman again fixed upon the tawdry cross of flowers, which were fast becoming wilted and lifeless, and I knew that she was still tormented by the comparison.

"Yours be prettier than mine," she said at last, breaking the silence between them.

The stout woman was still generous.

"Nonsense," she declared. "They baint at all. As I say, it's all in the first look. Them of yours will last for long days, them will."

The thin woman looked at her own flowers, still fresh in the wet newspaper about their stalks.

"Maybe," she said. "Maybe so. But folks like first

looks, they do. Yours—she'll be fair crazy over they. Well—there 'tis.''

IV

The bus neared Bath, descending the steep hills to the city, where Romans once built and bathed and ate, where Saxons had fought, and weavers had spun and woven, and half the literary men and women of England had later come in search of books. The Abbey bells were ringing as we swung past the terraces and the crescents with their eighteenth century houses.

Did she whose future must be brief have her compensations also? In the country expression which she had used in swift recognition of her disappointment were there perhaps concealed a larger recognition and assent? Was there, perhaps, a chance that with the wisdom bred in the hard, seemingly prescribed life of the country, she had learned without knowing that she had learned it, something of that freedom which acceptance brings the spirit?

The Immortals who had made the laws responsible for such simple words as hers still sat on their high thrones, even as we jostled one another in our own swaying seats.